M000204316

CORNERSTONES | VOL. 1
GOSPEL CULTURE

"Dr Joseph Boot seeks to bring the whole of the Christian tradition to bear on the whole world. Nothing is beyond the purview of the Gospel, and God's providence and purpose extend to every nook and cranny of the Cosmos, as well as to every area of life. This means affirmation and celebration of all that is according to the divine purpose, or is moving towards a fulfilment of it, and a critique of a world and human society gone wrong. A wrongness which the atoning God is sacrificially putting right. We need such rigour of thought and abundance of compassion in our engagement with cultures today. I look forward to the next volume."

RT REV. DR MICHAEL J. NAZIR-ALI
President, Oxford Centre for Training, Research, Advocacy and Training

"Cultural analysis purportedly reflecting a Christian perspective abounds these days. Unfortunately, most of it is: (a) inferior in content or argument; (b) compromised with pagan postmodernity; or (c) embarrassed at biblical truth, opting instead for natural theology. Conversely, what a breath of fresh air is this analysis by Dr. Joseph Boot. He is a rigorous thinker, uncompromisingly committed to biblical truth and unafraid to articulate it in the boldest way. He is a cultural theologian of the highest order. May God give us many more like him."

P. ANDREW SANDLIN, S.T.D., PH.D.
Founder and President, Center for Cultural Leadership
Coulterville, California, U.S.A.

CORNERSTONES | VOL. 1

GOSPEL CULTURE
LIVING IN GOD'S KINGDOM

JOSEPH BOOT

Wilberforce Publications
London

Copyright ©2016 Joseph Boot

The moral right of the author under the
Copyright, Designs and Patents Act 1988 has been asserted.

First published in Canada in 2016 by
Ezra Press

Second edition published in Great Britain in 2016 by
Wilberforce Publications Limited
70 Wimpole Street, London W1G 8AX
in association with the
Ezra Institute for Contemporary Christianity, Canada

All rights reserved.

Wilberforce Publications Limited is a wholly owned subsidiary of Christian Concern

No part of this publication may be reproduced or transmitted in any form or by any means, electronic or mechanical, including photocopy, recording or any information storage and retrieval system, without prior permission in writing from the publisher.

Unless otherwise indicated, Scripture quotations are from The Holy Bible, English Standard Version® (ESV®), copyright © 2001 by Crossway, a publishing ministry of Good News Publishers. Used by permission. All rights reserved.

Book design by Steve Oakley

Printed in the UK by Imprint Digital, Exeter
and worldwide by Createspace

ISBN 978-0-9956832-2-8

To Randall Currie
Christ's faithful servant and my friend

Contents

FOREWORD TO THE SECOND EDITION

In recent times in public life we have witnessed a number of dramatic events where the implausible happened, in part because of deep disillusion and alienation with the leaders the democratic systems of the West have thrown up.

How should a Christian reflect on that? I think the obvious question is to ask in what way these perceived shortcomings of the political classes make them different from the way the rest of the population behaves. We have a strongly self-centred culture; and the chaos in public life is because we have forgotten our Creator who makes all things new; who instructs how now we should live.

The Bible tells us that God is making all things new, that all things in heaven and on earth will be put under His feet and that He, in sending his son Jesus Christ, has come to redeem all things. The gospel, then, is not simply a message of salvation for the sinner but a cosmic plan of redemption for all creation.

The God of the Bible is invested in the world and everything in it. His Word, therefore, has something to say about the way we live our lives, run our countries and decide our laws. He is concerned with government, education, business, the arts, and all the cultural components which build our nation.

In this Cornerstones series Joe Boot intelligently challenges the relegation of the Christian faith to another truth among many, and gives us the language to speak out on what it really means for every element of society to flourish in the reality and full fruition of the gospel of the Lord Jesus Christ. For too long we have allowed the Church to be a refuge only and failed to equip one another to take our place in society to mould and shape public life. It is time to change.

ANDREA WILLIAMS
Chief Executive & Co-Founder,
Christian Concern & Christian Legal Centre

FOREWORD TO THE FIRST EDITION

Over thirty years ago, Francis Schaeffer asked a question that is still utterly imperative for the church to answer: "How should we then live?"[1] His answer was grounded in Scripture and theological reflection, and encompassed a wide array of topics from art and architecture to philosophy and poetry. Schaeffer rightly perceived that human beings are inevitably and always making cultures in every sphere of life they touch, whether it be in the realms of the fine arts and theology or in those of business and industry. Even more basic, Schaeffer knew that driving everything we do and think as human beings reflects a cultural worldview. And for Christians to effectively reach and engage men and women at any given time they need to know something of the culture of the very people they are seeking

---

[1] Francis Schaeffer, *How Should We Then Live? The Rise and Decline of Western Thought and Culture* (reprint; Wheaton: Crossway, 2005).

to reach. All of the great thinkers in the history of the Church have known this, from Paul and Augustine to Jonathan Edwards and B.B. Warfield.

In this new series of monographs by the British-Canadian Christian apologist and thinker Joe Boot, Francis Schaeffer's question will be considered and answered afresh. The *Cornerstones* series will seek to help twenty-first-century Christians interact in a scriptural manner with cultural trends, perspectives and presuppositions in every sphere of life, presenting a robust Christian critique and biblical defense. The gospel speaks to the entirety of human life and this series will accordingly seek to address all of this life "under the sun" with clarity.

Warmly recommended!

MICHAEL A.G. HAYKIN
Professor of Church History & Biblical Spirituality
The Southern Baptist Theological Seminary

PREFACE
TO THE SERIES

The Ezra Institute for Contemporary Christianity (EICC) is an evangelical Christian organization dedicated to two great objects. First, the preservation and advancement of the truth, freedom and beauty of the gospel, and second, the renewal of culture in terms of the lordship of Jesus Christ.

The gospel of the kingdom, resting as it does upon Christ's declaration of jubilee, is alone the source of true freedom, righteousness and justice. As well, the gospel is all-encompassing in scope, a leaven that permeates and informs every area of life and thought. Regarding this comprehensive truth of full salvation, Jesus himself declared, "If the Son sets you free, you shall be free indeed" (John 8:36).

Throughout history the Lord has entrusted the work of gospel-centred culture building and renewal to his people (Genesis 1:28; 9:1; Matthew 28:18–20). This task is particularly urgent in our day because the organs and institutions of modern culture have been thoroughly saturated by humanistic and pagan assumptions about the source and nature of truth and freedom. These pretensions have steadily redefined intellectual, social, familial, sexual and ethical norms, unleashing real evil and enslaving Western society in a radical opposition to Christ and the freedom brought by the gospel. From the school, academy and courthouse, to senates, parliaments and palaces, the Christian faith is being systematically expunged from public life and ignored or assaulted in our corridors of learning and power. If we love the gospel, our neighbours and freedom, Christians must take up the cultural task with faith and courage.

The EICC is committed to bringing a comprehensive gospel to bear on all of life, challenging and serving culture-shapers in all spheres, resourcing and equipping Christian leaders and professionals in public life and teaching believers to understand and advance the truth, beauty and freedom of the gospel in all its varied implications. By encouraging and intellectually resourcing Christian engagement with culture, we believe that biblical truth can once again captivate hearts and minds, and shape our future to the glory of God (Philippians 1:7; Colossians 1:15–20).

The *Cornerstones* series of short, focused monographs, published by Ezra Press, is intended to be an accessible point of entry for thoughtful Christians wishing to develop and/or strengthen their understanding of the scope and implications of the gospel, and of the particular but timeless challenges to that gospel being posed by non-Christian thought in the twenty-first century. From there, our hope is that this initiative will be further used of the Lord to animate, encourage and strengthen the public witness and testimony of God's church, so that she might live up to her calling as the pillar and support of the truth (1 Timothy 3:15), so that through the church, the manifold wisdom of God might be made known (Ephesians 3:10).

RANDALL CURRIE
Board Chair, Ezra Institute for Contemporary Christianity

GOSPEL CULTURE: WHY IT MATTERS

OF THE INCREASE OF HIS GOVERNMENT AND PEACE THERE
WILL BE NO END (ISAIAH 9:7).

THE CRISIS OF CULTURE

Commenting on the life and thought of Friedrich Nietzsche, G.K.
Chesterton set forth a universal truth, that "The man who thinks
without the proper first principles goes mad."[1] Madness would
increasingly seem to be the right term to describe the direction of
our culture today. Our first principles for the social order have clearly
ceased to be the Word of God and, tragically, that same Word is being
abandoned by large parts of the church itself. In its place, man's own
will is permitted to rule and determine truth and justice and thereby
the direction of culture. The insightful Canadian philosopher George

---

[1] G.K. Chesterton, *Orthodoxy* (1908, reprint; London: Booklassic, 2015), 20.

Grant understood the West's present cultural perspective well:

> Justice is understood to be something strictly human, having nothing to do with obedience to any divine command or conformity to any pattern "laid up in heaven." Moral principles, *like all other social conventions*, are something "made on earth." Human freedom requires that the principles of justice be the product of human agreement or consent, that is, they must be the result of a contract, and these principles must therefore be rooted in an understanding of the *interests of human beings* as individuals rather than in any sense of duty or obligation to anything above humanity. The terms of the contract may well *change as circumstances and interests change*. But the restraints free individuals accept must always be "horizontal" in character rather than "vertical."[2]

In this rejection of vertical accountability for horizontal relativity, modern man is conferring on himself the contractual *right* to redefine his gender irrespective of creational chromosomes; the *right* to murder (abortion); the *right* to polygamy, sodomy, bestiality or any sexual predilection; the *right* to suicide; the *right* to euthanize children and the elderly or sick; the *right* to homosexual "marriage"; the *right* to prostitution and pornography; the *right* to suppress worship of the living God and the free speech of Christians; the *right* to blasphemy and endless violations of Sabbath—all dressed in the garb of freedom and human dignity, which amounts to nothing but radical autonomy.

Thus today, few would deny that our Western moral principles are shifting like sand or that the metamorphosis of the church's relationship with the surrounding culture is happening before our eyes. The profoundly compromised character of much of the modern church is no secret. Liberalizers in both evangelical and mainline denominations love to publish their apostasy to the world in an effort to convince themselves that media coverage and approval from cultural elites mean approval and sanction from God. Since cultural circum-

---

[2] Hugh Donald Forbes, *George Grant: A Guide to His Thought* (Toronto: University of Toronto Press, 2007), 46–47.

stances change and moral truth is reduced to social convention by the contemporary muses, many of the leaders within our churches have long forsaken anything resembling a scriptural and historical understanding of our world-transforming faith. Consequently, understanding both the nature and relationship of the scriptural gospel to culture has never been more vital to the future of the Western church and the destiny of our world.

THE MEANING OF CULTURE

To gain a proper understanding of how the gospel relates to culture, we must begin by clarifying the meaning of culture itself. The English words *culture* and *agriculture* are derived from a Latin root (*colere*) and are related to *cultus* (worship). The direct association of culture with worship is most noticeable in our ongoing use of the word cult for various religions. Culture is perhaps best understood as the *public manifestation of the religious ground-motive (i.e. worship) of a people.* Culture is therefore a state of being cultivated by intellectual and moral tilling in terms of a prevailing *cultus* and, by natural extension, forms a particular type of civilization. This *cultus* is always communitarian and is transmitted through the family, education, law, art and other varied institutions shaping cultural life. As Herman Dooyeweerd points out, "The religious ground-motive of a culture can never be ascertained from the ideas and the personal faith of the *individual.* It is truly a communal motive that governs the individual even when one is not consciously aware of it or acknowledges it."[3]

To illustrate practically, if a person travels to Saudi Arabia, Syria or Pakistan, they experience Islamic culture—expressed in everything from law and education, to art and diet. If one goes to the major cities of India, there one experiences Hindu culture as the social order. In North Korea and China, one encounters Marxist-oriented cultures. The traveller in Tibet encounters Buddhist culture, and so forth. In the West today, we increasingly experience a humanistic, secular culture, deeply influenced by pagan spirituality, which at the same time displays the cultural vestiges of Christianity. The spiritual mainspring of Western culture has been undergoing a seismic shift

---

3 Herman Dooyeweerd, *Roots of Western Culture: Pagan, Secular and Christian Options*, trans. John Kraay, ed. D.F.M. Strauss (Grand Rapids: Paideia Press, 2012), 9.

for many years, so that Christian truth has largely ceased to give direction to the historical development of our society. This is a precarious place to be, for, at this point, "a real crisis emerges at the foundations of that society's culture. Such a crisis is always accompanied by spiritual uprootedness."[4] That radical uprooting is all around us. Henry Van Til thus accurately defined culture as "religion externalized."[5] All culture is the expression of a people's worship, in terms of which they cultivate their society.

THE DIRECTION OF CULTURE

In biblical categories, culture is what human beings make of *God's creation*. This is what our first parents were set in the garden to do as royal priests in God's cosmic temple—to subdue and develop all things under God and turn creation into a God-glorifying culture, cultivating everything in terms of his will and purpose as an act of worship. This command has never been rescinded. The Reformed theologian Herman Bavinck points out:

> Gen. 1:26 teaches us that God had a purpose in creating man in His image: namely that man should *have dominion....* If now we comprehend the force of this subduing (dominion) under the term of *culture...*we can say that *culture in its broadest sense is the purpose for which God created man after his image.*[6]

Culture-making is therefore inescapable for all God's image-bearers, for it is an expression of worship. Human beings will turn the visible and invisible materials of God's creation into culture, either as covenant keepers or covenant breakers, since all people are God's creatures and are either obedient or disobedient as they stand in relationship to God. This *antithesis* in cultural life is something Scripture clearly teaches. In Romans 1, Paul is explicit that there are ultimately only *two possible directions* for culture. These theological

---

4 Dooyeweerd, *Roots of Western Culture*, 9.

5 Henry R. Van Til, *The Calvinistic Concept of Culture* (Grand Rapids: Baker, 1972), 200. Emphasis added.

6 Herman Bavinck, "The Origin, Essence and Purpose of Man," in *Selected Shorter Works of Herman Bavinck*, ed. John Hendryx (West Linn, OR: Monergism Books, 2015), loc. 469.

alternatives are mutually exclusive. One rests upon *worship of the Creator*, the other upon *worship of creation*. The worship of any aspect of the creation is called *idolatry* in Scripture, and this leads to cultural decay. It follows then that there is no such thing as a neutral culture, for on this Pauline basis, no institution and no cultural activity can ever be religiously neutral.

It is true of course that Christians who worship the Creator and humanists who deny the Creator and worship one or more aspects of creation pursue many of the same cultural tasks. Both marry and build families, for example; both establish educational institutions; both make fine art, produce films and write music. However, though the *structure* of the musical notation remains the same for both, the *direction* of the music is different. In the same way, though the legal structure of the marriage will in many cases be the same, the directions of a Christian and non-Christian marriage are radically different. The *structure* of something concerns God's creational laws and ordained pattern that pertain to it—for example, with regard to the family, church, and state. Whereas the *direction* of these spheres concerns the religious orientation that they have. There are many structures in God's creation, but only *two directions*. We are either oriented toward God or toward idolatry in marriage, family, church, state, art, science and every other sphere. We will either seek to serve and glorify God in each area of life, or our lives will have an apostate direction, with no central place for God and his revelation.

I note this important distinction between *structure* and *direction*, because as Christians we recognize the reality of the Fall and hence the problem of sin in all human activities and institutions. Regarding marriage, for example, God's ordained *structure* for marriage is still the same as at creation, but the *direction* of the hearts of those in the marriage relationship is, when unregenerate, turned in an apostate direction. Likewise, the essential challenge of political life (as with family and church life) is not that God's ordained *structure of the state* is broken, but that many of those involved in politics have hearts, and thereby convictions and ideologies, that are hostile to God and his Word. To put this another way, when people opine that their marriage "failed," the Christian recognizes that it was not the God-given *structure of marriage* that failed, but rather that the problem lay in one or both of the hearts of the couple concerned, so that their relationship broke down. Likewise, with respect to the state, failed states do not lead us to conclude that God's ordination of the role of the state is at fault, but that various actors within the state failed, leading to its collapse. In short, socio-cultural and political challenges are, at root, fundamentally religious and moral challenges that centre in the heart of man.

THE TRANSFORMATION OF CULTURE

In view of all this, it is clear that implicit in the *Christian gospel* is a particular *vision of culture*—indeed, the gospel *is a culture*, because it is centred on the worship of the living God, through Jesus Christ, and the enthronement of Christ as Lord over the heart, mind, soul and strength of every believer. That the gospel forms a new culture is thus an inescapable deduction from the meaning of both terms. If culture is the public expression of the worship of a people, and the gospel restores man to true worship (i.e. of the Creator, not the creation), then the gospel restores man to *true culture*, which is the kingdom of God. Man was not made to live a fragmented and dissonant life, but was made an integral being, to worship and glorify God and have dominion, under God, in all things. The gospel fully restores man to his calling to worship and to serve, beginning with the regeneration of the heart of man and thereby effecting a radical change in the core of man's being.

Since the gospel effects such a great transformation, we must conclude that the dreary condition of our culture today is in large measure due to the apostasy of the church and Christian family from their respective callings. Since the so-called Enlightenment, Christians have steadily surrendered the various organs of culture—education, law, arts, charity, medicine, government—almost entirely to the increasingly humanistic state. We have progressively retreated into a pietistic bubble, concerned largely with eternal verities and keeping souls from hell, and we have faithlessly limited Christ's jurisdiction to the institutional church. The result has been the marginalization of the Christian church and a change of religion in the public sphere. Some freedoms for the gospel remain, though threatened. But history shows that freedoms not fought for are soon forfeited. If we love God and our neighbour, then a full-orbed gospel culture for all of life will be of great importance to us, not simply our inner piety. We will want to witness to the reality of our cosmos-renewing gospel and call people and nations to repentance and the life, joy, beauty and truth that is found in Jesus Christ and his rule alone.

This great concern for cultural transformation is found everywhere in Scripture. The Bible is filled with accounts of God's servants confronting sin, idolatry and all false worship, and thereby transforming kings, kingdoms and cultures with the truth.

- Moses had the temerity to confront Pharaoh—he did not complain to God that "spiritual" leaders shouldn't confront political leaders regarding political matters.
- The prophet Nathan confronted King David for his adultery. Elijah confronted Ahab for his lawlessness.
- Daniel confronted the pagan King Nebuchadnezzar until he acknowledged that "the Most High is sovereign over the kingdoms of men and gives them to anyone he wishes" (Daniel 4:25). Nebuchadnezzar was converted and declared of the Lord, that "his dominion is an everlasting dominion and his kingdom endures from generation to generation.... I Nebuchadnezzar, praise and extol and honor the king of heaven, for all his works are right and his ways are just" (Daniel 4:34, 37).
- Jonah dramatically confronted pagan Nineveh, which led to city-wide repentance from the monarch down.
- Amos prophesied against the surrounding pagan nations for violating God's law.
- Nehemiah petitioned the king of Persia for the return of the Jews to Jerusalem and found favour.
- Esther intervened with Xerxes on behalf of her people.
- John the Baptist confronted Herod for rejecting God's design for marriage.
- The apostle Peter confronted the Jewish Sanhedrin with the ultimate authority of Christ and his determination to obey God rather than men.
- The apostle Paul confronted the Athenian court, Felix, Festus and Agrippa, with Christ's lordship and his gospel.
- Jesus himself called Herod Antipas a fox and reminded Pilate that he had no authority, save what was given him from above.

Why should these servants of God have bothered with the socio-cultural order and its leaders? Why did they "interfere" with the political and cultural life of the nations? These great saints (and of course, the Lord above all in history) all dramatically impacted the culture of their time. A critical biblical clue to their motivation is given to us in Psalm 2, where the identity and authority of Christ is prophetically set forth:

Why do the nations rage
    and the peoples plot in vain?
The kings of the earth set themselves,
    and the rulers take counsel together,
    against the Lord and against his Anointed, saying,
"Let us burst their bonds apart
    and cast away their cords from us."
He who sits in the heavens laughs;
    the Lord holds them in derision.
Then he will speak to them in his wrath,
    and terrify them in his fury, saying,
"As for me, I have set my King
    on Zion, my holy hill."
I will tell of the decree:
The Lord said to me, "You are my Son;
    today I have begotten you.
Ask of me, and I will make the nations your heritage,
    and the ends of the earth your possession.
You shall break them with a rod of iron
    and dash them in pieces like a potter's vessel."
Now therefore, O kings, be wise;
    be warned, O rulers of the earth.
Serve the Lord with fear,
    and rejoice with trembling.
Kiss the Son,
    lest he be angry, and you perish in the way,
    for his wrath is quickly kindled.
Blessed are all who take refuge in him.

It is important to stress in our current church context, in light of texts such as this, that God does not hold a referendum on the identity and role of his Son. He is not dependent on majority support. The voice of the people *is not* the voice of God. God does not seek our approval of his absolute claims. Christ is King not because or when we accept it. His Word is not true only if kings or politicians or magistrates acknowledge it. Christ's Lordship is total, absolute, objective reality, irrespective of the desires and will of men. Nowhere in Scripture are national cultures, their kings and rulers, commanded to be *neutral* or impartial to various religious claims in the public space, as though man were judge over God. All men and all rulers are required to kiss the Son (acknowledge his authority) and submit to him. Scripture is very plain that all things are being made subject to Christ, in heaven and on earth (1 Corinthians 15:28; Colossians 1:15–20) and we are commanded to pray for his kingdom and will to be done on earth, as in heaven.

In sum, all worship, lordship and sovereignty either belong to Christ the creator and redeemer—the *transcendent* source of all truth to which we are all accountable—or the god concept is to be found *within creation*. I have argued that these are the two forms of worship in the world and therefore the two ultimate cultural choices. Chesterton correctly perceived the historical implications of this antithesis in the nations of the world:

> It is only by believing in God that we can ever criticize the government. Abolish God and the government becomes *the God*. That fact is written across all human history…wherever the people do not believe in something beyond the world, they will worship the world. But above all they *will worship the strongest thing in the world.*[7]

We will worship either the triune *Creator* or we will worship the *creature* by absolutizing some aspect of creation. Typically, as Scripture and history reveal, this has been man himself, embodied in the king, ruler or state. But the gospel tells us that Jesus Christ, as both

---

7 G.K. Chesterton, "Christendom in Dublin," in *The Collected Works of G.K. Chesterton*, Vol. 20 (San Francisco: Ignatius Press, 2001), 35–84, 57.

fully man and fully God, is sovereign Lord and that he alone is worthy of all worship, praise and glory. And so the prophet says, "of the increase of His government and peace, there shall be no end" (Isaiah 9:7). His resurrection life and power not only mean the transformation of all culture, they mean finally, that all men and nations shall bow at the feet of Jesus (Philippians 2:10–11).

2

THE DEATH OF MAN AND CRISIS OF THE SOCIAL ORDER

BUT HE WHO SINS AGAINST ME WRONGS HIS OWN SOUL;
ALL THOSE WHO HATE ME LOVE DEATH (PROVERBS 8:36).

In the previous chapter, we saw that as Western culture has pursued a course away from the God of Scripture and his Word-revelation, we have not ceased to worship, but have merely exchanged true worship for idolatry in socio-cultural life—from law and politics, to education and art. This change has essentially been a quiet cultural revolution, the fruits of which are now being clearly manifested. In this chapter, I want to analyze the present cultural decay and the existential confusion arising from our idolatrous turn.

SPIRITUAL NIHILISM
In the 1960s, movements began in earnest to remove Scripture and prayer from public schools in the United States and Canada, striking

at the *vulnerable soul* of these nations seated at small tables to learn in innocence. In Canada in 1985, under the *Charter*, the last vestiges of public Christian identity were abolished in Ontario, as the Lord's Prayer was banned from schools as unconstitutional. The result has been the steady moral neutering of two generations, and the casting adrift of the *human personality*. It has led to the absolutization of the *feeling* aspect of human experience, so that now, in a plastic world, "I feel, therefore, I am."

Under the influence of European radicals like Michel Foucault, we have been told that there is no essential self; the human person and the human family are merely social constructs. We are what we make and define ourselves to be.[1] In such a cosmos, even grammar and pronouns must go, since they speak of law and norms. Man is little more than artifice and is bound by nothing outside or beyond himself.

By contrast, at the foundation of a scriptural philosophy of life, we discover the most fundamental aspect of God's Word-revelation for granting a coherent and intelligible vision of the human person:

> Then God said, "Let us make man in our image, after our like-ness. And let them have dominion over the fish of the sea and over the birds of the heavens and over the livestock and over all the earth and over every creeping thing that creeps on the earth." So God created man in his own image, in the image of God he created him; male and female he created them (Genesis 1:26–27).

There is no parallel to this starting point anywhere else in human thought. The triune God of Scripture creates all things out of noth-ing—all that is distinct from himself—and makes the human person in his image, where the "I" or human ego is established as a transcen-dent reference point for all aspects of temporal human experience. That is to say, the human "I" (or heart) cannot be reduced to any single aspect of created reality. Although a part of creation, man somehow transcends nature. As Blaise Pascal so well understood, the

---

[1] See Jim Miller, *The Passion of Michel Foucault* (New York: Simon & Schuster, 1993).

human person is a mystery that transcends his environment[2] as a living, *integral being*, comprehensible only with reference back to the living God as the source and origin of all life, law, truth and meaning. This unique human identity and the critically important distinction between creator and creature imply, of necessity, a limit to both the reach of human thought (as rooted in our temporal experience) and the legislative prerogatives of man. We read in the book of Ecclesiastes, "As you do not know the way the spirit comes to the bones in the womb of a woman with child, so you do not know the work of God who makes everything" (Ecclesiastes 11:5).

The average person today, however, has lost sight of the true nature of man as God's creature and fallen prey to spiritual nihilism and a world of negation that they were taught to embrace by their instructors. As the great Dutch philosopher Herman Dooyeweerd put it regarding modern man, "He has lost all his faith and denies any higher ideals than the satisfaction of his desires…. To him, God is dead…modern mass-man has lost himself and considers himself cast into a world that is meaningless."[3] In his hit single "If I Ever Lose My Faith in You," the singer-songwriter-poet Sting gives expression to the existential rootlessness of an ailing humanity. He describes himself as "a lost man in a lost world," having lost all faith in science, progress, politics and the church.[4]

As a result of this modern temper, there has perhaps never been a time in the past fifteen centuries or more when the Western world faced a greater crisis of identity and thereby confronted so dramatically its own social and cultural ruin. Any observant and thinking Christian can see that we are a radically uprooted and dislocated generation, adrift in the world. Social and cultural philosophers, commentators and theologians have spilt much ink seeking to trace upstream to the font of the problem, following the various tributaries of the crisis toward its common source, but not all have grasped the *religious character* of its subterranean spring. That common source is the decline of the human personality via the apostasy of the heart from

---

[2] See Blaise Pascal, *The Thoughts of Blaise Pascal* (Westport, Conn: Greenwood Press, 1978).

[3] Herman Dooyeweerd, *In the Twilight of Western Thought* (Grand Rapids: Paideia Press, 2012), 120.

[4] Sting, "Ten Summoner's Tales" (Hollywood: A&M Records, 1993).

God and the consequent emergence of *mass-man* (i.e. depersonalized, dispensable human beings) in a technocratic society where the individual strives to "find himself" without God. Not many perceive that our present situation is so precarious that the elegy of Western culture is on the verge of being composed.

WHAT IS MAN?

We see examples daily in the media of people in the grip of a *radical relativism,* unimaginable even twenty-five years ago. As abstracted and generalized people reduced to self-created group identities, we no longer know *what a human being is.* This condition has advanced to such a degree that we are essentially unsure if there are any human norms that transcend radical autonomous desire and subjective self-identification. We are not even confident of the intrinsic value of the human person made in God's image, whether pre-born, new-born, disabled, aging, sick or despairing. Indeed, we are so fundamentally uprooted that we are no longer assured of the scientific and chromosomal reality of the binary gender distinctions of male and female, of normative human sexuality, or of the oldest institutions known to the human race—marriage and family.

Our profound confusion today is such that some people are not even sure that they occupy the right age group or gender, were born into the right people group, or even gestated by the right species, since they "feel" like something else. No one dares to challenge these inner fictions, since all that is left of the human personality is the notion that autonomous and subjective feeling has the *absolute existence* of God himself. As such, there is no longer a basis for differentiation of any objective kind. And thus, in a world mired in the irrational fluidity of all things, where the possibility of normative differentiation between truth and falsehood, right and wrong, reality and unreality, has collapsed, culture has not simply reached a bump in the road, but has been sucked into a kind of vortex of democratic insanity, spiralling toward what Cornelius Van Til called "disintegration into the void."[5]

In our disarticulated world, the vain rantings of Nietzsche's over-

---

5 Cited in R.J. Rushdoony, *Genesis,* Commentaries on the Pentateuch (Vallecito, CA: Chalcedon Foundation, 2002), 3.

men, who have gone *beyond good and evil*, declare the reasonable and sane to be sick, mad or malevolent and demand that the voice of plain reason be silenced in the face of the cultural conjurers' reimagining of the world. The stark reality of our situation is that we are facing the *death of man as man* in the West. By denying, debunking and defacing the image of God in man we are losing our very soul (Matthew 16:26).

Jesus Christ said: "For what will it profit a man if he gains the whole world and forfeits his soul? Or what shall a man give in return for his soul?" (Matthew 16:26). When iconoclastic and fractious man declares that what is left of human dignity is now rooted solely in *radical autonomy* from God, revelation, true human community and all familial and moral obligation, then we have realized the most fundamental atomization and depersonalization of all life. Such a society, whatever its protest to the contrary, is *anti-social* to the core, whilst, ironically, individual *responsibility* for action and its consequences is passed on to an impersonal, scientific society governed by statistics, bureaucracy, fashion, technology, social planning and other dehumanizing forces. The socio-cultural deficit ensuing from this disaster cannot be fixed with any amount of state welfare or scientific planning—there is no *technical solution* to this colossal religious problem.

In the state of crisis that results from the illusion of the *creative freedom of selfhood*, people are often *deeply, inwardly afraid*, even as they revel in an autonomy that finds endless social indulgence and legal sanction. People on every side are gripped by sadness, fear, guilt and despair that no amount of psychotropic prescriptions can finally ameliorate or truly heal—by such methods the fear of disintegration and death is simply supressed. But, as Dooyeweerd rightly noted, "It is uncomprehended revelation of God that fills humankind with fear and trembling."[6]

We may deny God, and man as his *image bearer*, pressing ahead in a suicidal course, but this always proves to be pure vanity, for we are surrounded inside and out by the reality of God and his order. This revelation may well be supressed, but it is inescapable and still grips

---

[6] Herman Dooyeweerd, *Roots of Western Culture* (Grand Rapids: Paideia Press, 2012), 101.

the being of every person, generating both guilt and deep disquiet. Consequently, there is no recovery for our society till we recognize that, whatever our gains materially, we have *lost our soul*—and for this Christ warns us that there is a reckoning, for "God is not mocked; what a man sows, he reaps" (Galatians 6:7). Our only recourse is true repentance, both personal and national.

NATURE RELIGION

In the meantime, our culture looks to political and indeed *magical solutions* to its ills, because, as one Christian thinker puts it, "The truth is so intolerable to fallen humanity that even when it does take hold of people, they still seek to escape its total claims in every possible way."[7] Into this increasingly pretentious and arrogantly over-reaching world of cultural and political life, God has called Christians to be the leaven of Christ, to serve God and minister life and hope to our fellow man in the public space—if only at times through a kind of prophetic witness to those in authority.

In this task, Christians must recognize that all of life—including cultural life—is shaped by the beliefs, or more properly the *religious worldviews*, of those who participate in it—and I have already described some of the fruits of the religious worldview that increasingly dominates our culture. I say *religious* worldview, because man is a worshipping being. We saw in the previous chapter that Paul makes clear, in his letter to the Romans, that if we refuse to worship the living, creator God, we do not cease to worship. Rather we will worship *some aspect of creation itself*—some being or thing will be absolutized. This the Christian calls idolatry, apostasy from the true God, finding its root in the human heart and spreading out to touch everything. Before renewal of a Christian view of culture is possible, a self-conscious appreciation of the depths to which we have fallen is necessary.

Today we are clearly in the grip of God's historical judgements, seen in our growing adherence to very ancient beliefs dressed in new outfits. Anthropologists in the past called them "mana beliefs," which lay at the foundation of the disintegration of the human personality in pagan cultures. These beliefs are characterized by a supposed

---

7 Dooyeweerd, *Roots of Western Culture*, 109.

fluidity of reality between the *personal and impersonal* (the hallmark of a nature religion), for *mana* is believed to be a mysterious life force that underlies everything. Millions of people in our culture (often unwittingly) pay homage to such a life force, from the yoga mat and alternative healer, to the science classroom, where nature is deified as an *endless stream of life* that spontaneously evolved from an original mysterious point of *undifferentiated absolute unity*. It was such a belief that filled the ancient Greco-Roman world with dread in the face of blind fate, and so promoted the *nobility of suicide*—a belief re-emergent in our time.

When nature itself is, in various ways, *absolutized*, culture becomes increasingly decrepit, because with all of nature being somehow an aspect of the *divine*, emerging from an original unity, how can real and meaningful differentiation take place at the familial, biological, ethical, artistic, juridical, moral or even ontological level? In such a view, man—and his culture—is merely impermanent artifice in a mysterious fluidity. And, in the post-Darwinian world that we occupy, we can no longer speak cogently or persuasively of even "natural law" as a moral referent in the way that the pseudo-Christian secularists of past generations did, for we no longer know what "nature" is. A mysterious world of chaotic forces can give no objective or transcendent law, and so all that is left to the *mana* world of jurisprudence is *positive law*, which emerges as a *development of the reflective experience of the people*, as Oliver Wendell Holmes Jr., former Chief Justice of the U.S. Supreme Court and leading legal thinker, argued.[8] The obvious question is: *Who will interpret* the reflective experience of the people and transform experience into law? Increasingly, the answer is a new elite in our courts, cut loose from accountability to God and Scripture's definition of man as God's image-bearer.

POLITICAL SALVATION AND THE NEW PRIESTHOOD

This new elite or humanist priesthood (Plato's philosopher kings) is necessary, of course, because social chaos is not a workable *political philosophy*, and in a lawless world of radical autonomy, humanity needs *salvation* from all those fatalistic forces threatening to crush

---

8   R.J. Rushdoony, *Law and Liberty* (Vallecito, CA: Ross House Books, 2009), 28–29.

it. Increasingly, our society looks to *absolutize the cultural sphere of the state* as the agency that should be able to control the threat that man, as an aspect of nature, is to himself. It is to the state therefore that idolatrous man largely *delegates* his freedom.

It naturally follows that modern political doctrine rests, typically, on a set of beliefs that flatly contradict what God says about humanity. It is not that our culture denies that there is evil in the world, but we refuse to locate that evil in the heart of man (who is thought of as inherently good and perfectible), blaming instead the environment and spheres of social order like the family, the church and private property, as well as other structures of alleged inequality that supposedly war against an original equality and unity in the human race.

Fairly recently, I was a fly on the wall in a Labour Party committee meeting in the Parliament buildings in London, during which they were analyzing their serious defeat in the 2016 British general election. One MP and key speaker began his presentation by saying that the core problem is that the Labour Party needs a robust return to the conviction of the *essential goodness* of man. This illustrated the recurrent theological-political illusion concerning the human person: people are *born without sin*, and so we can change people by doing away with the evil in society by getting back to an unspoiled condition that humanity supposedly lived in in his primitive past—a condition of absolute social equality. So, if we abolish marriage and the family, no one will be subject to *hierarchy* anymore and women and children will not *feel* subjugated. If we eliminate binary gender norms, no one will *feel* oppressed by distinctions anymore. If we eliminate income inequality, no one will be greedy anymore. If we open our borders and embrace Islamists returning from fighting with ISIS and find them money and housing, they won't want to crucify and behead Christians anymore or plot against our country. In this view, human beings are perfectible by *political technique*—a repackaged world of magic.

In this erroneous view our unfallen nature is not fixed, but *plastic*. We are not beings made in God's image, who have *fallen into sin and idolatry*, who need to be restrained from evil by revealed moral law and renewed by Jesus Christ and God's Holy Spirit. In fact, we are so malleable that we may become *trans-human* or *post-human*, not only by redefining ourselves, but also by evolving to merge with our own technology. This is a world of political and technocratic magic, resting on *mana beliefs*, which hold we can abolish sin, guilt, poverty, disease, indolence, ignorance, hunger and even death itself, so long as God and man as his image-bearer can be removed as roadblocks. The key obstacle is *all hierarchy* (except the privilege of belonging to a new cultural elite), because the principle of hierarchy is a reminder of the distinction between man and God.

In this great levelling process, God is thought to be brought down to the level of man, and man raised to the level of God. If the authority of families, parents, the church, pastors, private businesses, guilds and associations are eroded, if there can be an abolition of all true authority outside the political elite and its legislative apparatus, which authoritatively *interprets the experience* of the people, perhaps we can abolish God himself, who stands behind and over all legitimate authority. Critically, centralization and massive political power must be accrued to the state do this. This path, it is held, is *true liberation* for the human personality. The cultural theologian Andrew Sandlin has summarized it like this:

Liberals [progressives] since the French Revolution have engaged in one massive liberation project, what has been called "the oppression-liberation nexus." The liberal religion has become one of never-ending clawing for the liberation of humanity from every tyranny—real or imagined: the secularists must be liberated from the religionists, the parishioners from the clergy, the enlightened from the unenlightened, the citizens from royalty, the poor from the rich, the workers from the capitalists, blacks from whites, women from men, wives from husbands, children from parents, debtors from creditors, employees from employers, homosexuals from heterosexuals, convicts from law abiding citizens—and soon, if the trajectory persists, polygamists from monogamists and pedophiles from prison guards. The Great Liberation now extends even to non-human nature: the liberation of "the environment" from rapacious humanity.[9]

---

9 Andrew Sandlin, *Political Liberalism: Theological Presuppositions* (Coulterville, CA: Centre for Cultural Leadership, 2015), 16.

The social cost and destructiveness of this autonomous liberation project, led by the political priesthood, is beyond full comprehension, and the welfare states of Europe and, increasingly, North America are now buckling under the financial reality of such a counterfeit Exodus.

If the human race had adequately learned anything by now from our historical experience, it should have been that our rejection of God and the *image of God* in man leads to the *endless defacing and destruction of that image* and the steady decay of diverse cultural life, as the political sphere overreaches itself to try to play a messianic role in people's lives. *As man kills himself and his fellow man as God's image-bearer*, he languishes in the ruins of a social order that cannot find a solution to its malady from within nature itself. Simply put, human beings cannot be remade or renewed by technique and will never be perfected until Christ establishes his kingdom in all its fullness.

The contemporary religious illusion that the human ego has the same *absolute existence* as God himself is a direct succumbing to the original lie proffered to our first parents: "Ye shall be as gods" (Genesis 3:5, KJV). In both seeking "himself" and his "god" in the temporal world of experience, modern man has *lost himself in the abyss, absolutizing* that which is in fact *relative*—and thereby comprehensible only in reference back to our Creator, revealed to us in the person of Christ. This incalculable loss and radical spiritual uprooting together form the foundation of our current crisis, which presently shows no sign of abating.

THE DEFINING WORD OF GOD

In clear contrast to contemporary political illusions, Scripture tells us that the human "I" (person) is *nothing in and of itself*, but truly lives only in reference to the creative power and defining Word of God. Indeed, true knowledge of ourselves is dependent, as John Calvin made clear, on true knowledge of God.[10] The foundation of all true

---

[10] See John Calvin, *Institutes of the Christian Religion* 1.1.1, trans. Henry Beveridge (London: Arnold Hatfield, for Bonham Norton, 1599); http://www.ccel.org/c/calvin/institutes/institutes.html; accessed July 22, 2016.

knowledge of God is right relationship with God—in short, the love of God! The first commandment is to love the Lord our God with heart, mind, soul and strength (Deuteronomy 6:5; Matthew 22:37), and since God is to be so wholeheartedly loved, his *image-bearer* will of necessity be loved also, which is the second commandment—to love our neighbour as ourselves. Nowhere in the Christian view can such love lead to the destruction of that image in gender-fluid confusion, the redefinition of God's creational institution of marriage or the murder of our neighbour in the womb or—in the name of autonomy and dignity—in age, sickness or despair.

The simple truth is that, without *love for God* and a recognition of his Word-revelation to us in Christ and in Scripture, we are not only unable truly to love our neighbour, we cannot even identify them truly. We find, in fact, that we cannot answer a most elementary question: "What is a person?"

Herman Dooyeweerd cuts to the heart of the matter:

The question: "What is man? Who is he?" cannot be answered by man himself. However, it has been answered by God's word-revelation, which uncovers the religious root and centre of human nature in its creation, fall into sin and redemption by Jesus Christ. Man lost true self-knowledge when he lost the true knowledge of God. But all idols of the human selfhood, which man in his apostasy has devised, break down when they are confronted with the Word of God which unmasks their vanity and nothingness. It is this word alone which, by its radical grip, can bring about a real reformation of our view of man and of our view of the temporal world.[11]

In possession of this Word and, with it, a true knowledge of God and the human person, we are then able to pursue and build *true culture*—and *true community*. With a transcendent referent for life and thought, political and cultural reality can proceed faithfully in their various spheres, grounded in a true understanding of the life of humankind. The true Word reveals that human beings are *not* merged with *divinity*, a primitive life force, where law and social order are

---

[11] Dooyweerd, *In the Twilight of Western Thought*, 132.

merely an *emergent property* of nature manifest through man and where history must be captured by the man-gods to create a world community—the parliament of man.[12] That idolatrous vision requires *coerced collectivization* in an attempt to realize community, but in the process only undermines both true community and the individual. As one cultural theologian notes, "The more social distinctions are denied, the more force is required in society to bring men together, and the more force prevails in a society, the less communion."[13] In the Christian view, true community and communion rest on an *inner bond*, the grace of God, and then loyalty to God and his life and freedom-bringing Word.

In pursuit of a true and beautiful cultural life, we are dependent upon God's grace and the working of his Spirit, as we seek to oppose and defeat an apostate and destructive religious worldview that is ruining countless lives. We are called in this task to *love and thoughtful obedience*. And we can be confident of victory in the long run in this battle, because *an apostate culture of death has no future* against the Lord of life.

We must continue to serve the cause of Christ to the best of our ability, praying for those in authority, seeking the good of our fellow men, prophetically witnessing against idolatry in its varied forms and pursuing righteousness, truth, beauty and justice in every sphere of life. We will not always be loved for this stand, but this is the victory that overcomes the world—even our faith (1 John 5:4).

With an apostate heart, for almost a century, our culture has been progressively pursuing *the death of man as man* (i.e., God's image-bearer) and so we are surrounded by dead men—dead in trespasses and sins (Ephesians 2:1–5). But the Lord Jesus Christ assures us, "An hour is coming, and is now here, when the dead will hear the voice of the Son of God, and those who hear will live" (John 5:25).

Jesus Christ is life. This is our confidence.

---

[12] See Paul Kennedy, *The Parliament of Man: The Past, Present, and Future of the United Nations* (New York: Random House, 2007), taken from Tennyson's poem of the same name.

[13] R.J. Rushdoony, *The Foundations of Social Order*, 3rd ed. (Vallecito, CA: Ross House, 1998), 160.

3

THE POWER MOTIVE OF HUMANISTIC CULTURE

AND YOU HE MADE ALIVE, WHO WERE DEAD IN TRESPASSES AND SINS, IN WHICH YOU ONCE WALKED ACCORDING TO THE COURSE OF THIS WORLD, ACCORDING TO THE PRINCE OF THE POWER OF THE AIR, THE SPIRIT WHO NOW WORKS IN THE SONS OF DISOBEDIENCE (EPHESIANS 2:1–2).

So far in our study, we have considered the meaning of culture and its inescapably religious foundation. We have also briefly analyzed the crisis manifest in Western culture today and some of its social fruit; a crisis flowing from the fundamental abandonment of the Christian view of the human person as a creature made in God's image. This abandonment has led to a radical spiritual uprooting and existential confusion, seen all around us within the various organs of culture. Alongside of this, we are seeing the proliferation of pagan and occult spiritual ideas and practices as an alternative to the

Christian faith. In this chapter, I want to drill down further into the basic religious motive that lies at the root of the newly dominant Western worldview—a perspective that is driving the seismic changes in our culture.

MAGICIANS AND MATERIALISTS

In the preface to his imaginative novella, *The Screwtape Letters*, in which a senior devil advises a junior devil (Wormwood) in the art of deception, C.S. Lewis writes:

> There are two equal and opposite errors into which our race can fall about the devils. One is to disbelieve in their existence. The other is to believe, and to feel an excessive and unhealthy interest in them. They themselves are equally pleased by both errors and hail a materialist or a magician with the same delight.[1]

It is, I think, uncontroversial to say that the Western church in the twentieth century tended to fall, at least practically, if not theoretically, into the error of the materialist more than that of the magician. Certainly, old Protestant liberalism was concerned to reject many of the supernatural elements of the faith and reduce a personal devil to the realm of mythology. In recent decades, however, with the rise of new brands of liberalism in tandem with the progressive re-paganization of Western culture, the *worldview of witchcraft* is making a definitive comeback, as evidenced by a deeply unhealthy interest in occult beliefs and practices reappearing in academic and popular culture.[2] In speaking of the "worldview of witchcraft" I do not mean to suggest that our culture-shapers are all self-consciously engaged in occult practices. What I mean is that the essential worldview of the ancient world, which gave rise to various pagan ideas, arts and practices, has returned to us in slightly modified form.

Lewis was of course right to note that the materialist is caught in as great an error as the magician, since both positions are rooted in rebellion against God, both are diabolic and leave their presumptu-

---

[1]   C.S. Lewis, *The Screwtape Letters: Letters from a Senior to a Junior Devil* (Glasgow: Fount Paperbacks, 1982), 9.

[2]   See Peter Jones, *The Gnostic Empire Strikes Back* (Phillipsburg: P & R Publishing, 1992).

ous adherents exposed to real evil. The Scriptures reassure the Christian with regard to the devil and all his works, "You are from God little children, and you have conquered them, because the One who is in you is greater than the one who is in the world" (1 John 4:4). The apostle John goes on to affirm that those who do not listen to God's Word are in error regarding all spiritual matters, for "from this we know the Spirit of truth and the spirit of deception" (1 John 4:6). God's Word, not human research, must be our foundation as we grapple with the meaning and significance of humanistic religious motives.

THE BEGINNINGS OF DEVILRY

The Bible makes plain that there is a real archenemy of the Christian and the gospel: the adversary, called Satan or the devil. Jesus refers to his fall (Luke 10:18) and his kingdom (Matthew 12:26), identifying the character of the evil one and his martial strategy—murder and lies: "He was a murderer *from the beginning* and has not stood in the truth, because there is no truth in him. When he tells a lie, he speaks from his own nature, because he is a liar and the father of lies" (John 8:44).

Moreover, Satan's work is likened to that of a thief who comes "to steal and to kill and to destroy" (John 10:10). Death, robbery and deception are at the root of the worldview of witchcraft. Jesus is clear that lies and murder were on Satan's mind from the *beginning*. This "beginning" is a plain reference to the Garden of Eden, where God made man, male and female, in his own image and likeness (Genesis 1:1–27). Because of his hatred of God, the adversary wanted to *destroy man as man*—that is, as God had made him as the divine image-bearer—and after seeing mankind cursed to return to the dust, Satan provoked the first human murder—of Abel by his brother Cain (1 John 3:12). Clearly, Satan was—and is—a rebel against God, and the primordial crime he incited embroiled the human race in his rebellion, which centred around *denying* that man is created in God's image—with capacity for holiness, righteousness and dominion (power) on the finite level. In fact, we might say that man's revolt was seeded by the demonic lie that man is not actually a creature made in the *image* of God but is rather in process of *becoming* a god: "You will be like God, knowing [i.e. determining] good and evil" (Genesis 3:5). Thus, from the beginning,

Satan's word was a lie, a word of negation and a denial of God's creation and purpose:

God in jealousy seeks to prevent man from realizing himself. This self-realization Satan claimed to have, and his offer to Eve was precisely an opportunity for mankind to recreate itself in a new image, an image divorced from God and based entirely on man's creative will.... The nature and psychology of man thus cannot be understood without a realization that man, created in the image of God, is now trying to abolish that creation and to institute a new and satanic creation.[3]

From the beginning, Satan wanted humanity to join his project—to oppose God—and to build an order in which men are subordinate gods and servants to the dark lord—the evil one—a theme powerfully set forth in J.R.R. Tolkien's epic, *The Lord of the Rings*. In sum, to be human in the diabolic scheme meant *independence* from God and remaking oneself as, essentially, a new god. God's original design—for human beings to pursue true wisdom and godly power to work, serve and subdue all things in terms of the rule of the triune and sovereign Creator—had been corrupted. The new human pursuit became a quest for an *autonomous* knowledge, wisdom and power—godless resources that could be used to create a new man and a new world in light of the satanic plan of negation, opposing the living God by parodying his creation and kingdom.

We see in Scripture that our mother Eve, in the grip of demonic deception, thought that *rebellion* against God's Word "was desirable for obtaining wisdom" (Genesis 3:6). Hence, the self-realization that our first parents sought was autonomous knowledge and power that excluded the living God. It is for this reason that Scripture is clear: "Rebellion is like the sin of divination...because you have rejected the word of the Lord" (1 Samuel 15:23). It is no surprise then that King Saul, disqualified as king for his rebellion against the Lord, is soon consulting a medium at Endor, in search of an alternate word and knowledge from the spirit world.

---

3 R.J. Rushdoony, *Revolt against Maturity* (Vallecito, CA: Ross House Books, 1987), 60, 67.

We can say then that the foundation of all devilry is *rebellion* against God, which seeks knowledge, power and dominion through a negation of God's Word and purpose—this is the essence of the magical worldview. As such, there is no "white" or "good" magic. Any attempt to deny and overturn God's creative Word and divine purpose and to lawlessly manipulate circumstances to bend to my will, whether by spiritual powers and forces or by various political means, is a form of witchcraft, and evil on its face. At root, witchcraft implicitly involves the attempted remaking of man as a god with an autonomous source of knowledge and power, which is, in the final analysis, demonic. Now, since this is God's world and creation and cannot be overturned by *the lie*, the fiendish parodying of God requires endless manipulations, deceptions and the constant defacing of God's image-bearer, in order to seek to make the devil's illusions a social "reality."

THE UBIQUITY OF SORCERY

The strategies, arrangements and methods of witchcraft then, take many forms. It is neither rare nor a primitive phenomenon—the domain solely of antiquarians—but has been commonplace in all societies, in diverse appearances, throughout the centuries. I have suggested that the worldview that undergirds it has enjoyed a resurgence in recent decades. It is not incidental that the triumph of secularism in the public space has led to the growth of occultism and paganism in the private. C.S. Lewis pointed decades ago to a fundamental religious shift in the West, one which I would describe as clearly moving toward the pantheistic—toward the worldview of witchcraft:

We who defend Christianity find ourselves constantly opposed not by the *irreligion* of our hearers but by their *real religion*. Speak about beauty, truth and goodness, or about a God who is simply the indwelling principle of these three, speak about a great spiritual force pervading all things, a common mind of which we are all parts, a pool of generalized spirituality to which we can all flow, and you will command friendly interest. But the temperature drops as soon as you mention a God who has purposes and performs particular actions, who does one thing and not another, a concrete, choosing, commanding, prohibiting God with a determinate character. People become embarrassed or angry.[4]

This rejection of the personal, speaking and commanding God in educational, cultural and public life leads people to seek out alternate sources of spirituality, power and knowledge for living. As a result, various forms of occultism and witchcraft are becoming socially acceptable, celebrated and given credence as valid expressions of spirituality. In 1951, laws against witchcraft in England were repealed, granting more space for the discussion and practice of all manner of occult and magic arts. So ubiquitous are these practices now that many hapless Westerners do not even realize that they are taking part in them.

Some forms of primitive occult practice seek to engage spirits or demons directly to raise tables, levitate or move a glass on an Ouija board, but for the most part the rituals of witchcraft, from Hindu meditation to the Wiccan's coven, are directed toward nature-based divinities, primarily goddess worship. This is not due to any notion of a moral or personal relationship to a deity, but is a personification of an impersonal nature or "pure spirit," of which man himself is a part—that is, man is asserting himself as his *own god*. Thus, we should not be surprised to discover what researcher Linda Harvey has noted in regard to the goals of the witches' coven:

Ultimately...the practitioner *worships the self*, whose instincts and desires are empowered by occult spiritual forces. The focus of witchcraft is to take control of one's own (or another's) life. The enlightened witch invokes the goddess of choice...at the height of the ritual, there is an intense feeling of spiritual power, when the priestess believes she becomes one with the goddess and nature/earth.... The *godhood of self* is a stated pillar of witchcraft, as expressed in the 1974 Principles of Wiccan Belief, adopted by the council of American Witches. The introduction states: "We are not bound by traditions from other times and

---

[4] C.S. Lewis, *The Business of Heaven: Daily Readings*, ed. Walter Hooper (Glasgow: Fount, 1984), 31–32.

other cultures, and owe no allegiance to any person or power greater than the Divinity manifest through our own being."[5]

Harvey also points to the widespread resurgence of witchcraft, highlighting that, as far back as 1986, three Wiccan priestesses held faculty positions at Harvard Divinity School, an institution established in the seventeenth century to prepare men for Christian pastoral ministry.[6]

Although modern sorcery and occult arts are varied and inconsistent—they include everything from primitive dancing and sex acts (to induce rain or fertility), voodoo dolls, spells and talismans, to very elaborate enacted rites and rituals in covens, as well as various alternative healing practices proffered as science[7]—all teach that some sort of mystic *correspondence* exists between the metaphysical realm and the material world, so that the manipulation of forces or energy or powers to bring about man's will requires some corresponding action, technique or drama on earth. Without a detailed study of these numerous forms, how might we yet understand the relevance and power of the magical worldview today and its impact on our society?

PHILOSOPHICAL FOUNDATIONS OF MAGIC

We have seen from Scripture the implicit objective of witchcraft or magic arts, as well as their moral root—the desire of the practitioner to *become a god* with autonomous knowledge and power, grounded in overt rebellion. Behind this rebellion lie the powers of darkness. Paul is clear that the Christian is thus in a battle, not against flesh and blood, "but against the rulers, against the authorities, against the world powers of this darkness, against spiritual forces of evil in the heavens" (Ephesians 6:12). Their malevolent stratagem, however, is typically to disguise their evil as enlightenment (2 Corinthians 11:14). Not surprisingly, therefore, satanic strongholds are more often than not erected in areas of human philosophical thought and speculation

---

5 Linda Harvey, "The Global Mainstreaming of Witchcraft," in *On Global Wizardry: Techniques of Pagan Spirituality and a Christian Response*, ed. Peter Jones (Escondido, CA: Main Entry, 2010), 44–45.

6 Harvey, "The Global Mainstreaming of Witchcraft," 47.

7 See Candy Gunther Brown, *The Healing Gods: Complementary and Alternative Medicine in Christian America* (New York: Oxford University Press, 2013).

masquerading as wisdom. So the apostle writes, "The weapons of our warfare are not worldly, but are powerful through God for the demolition of strongholds. We demolish arguments and every high-minded thing that is raised up against the knowledge of God, taking every thought captive to obey Christ" (2 Corinthians 10:4–6).

In the ancient world, the founder of high magic was thought to be the mysterious personage of Zoroaster, as well as his religious disciples. These were the caste of "wise men" or "magi" who were essentially priests for the Persian Crown (ca. 600 B.C.). They helped spread the religion of Mithraism to the Roman Empire. Philosophically they were dualists, who posited conflicting powers of light and darkness, good and evil—Ahura Mazda and Ahriman, respectively. The *magi* (from whence we derive the words *magus, magician* and *magic*) offered sacrifices to both powers or personages, in order to appease the lord of darkness and bring about the good, and the Greeks and Romans believed the magi not only to be wise, but capable of incredible feats and miracles. Critically, the magi professed to be able to communicate with the gods and to foretell the future.[8]

Note here again that an autonomous knowledge of events and spiritual power were both associated with the magi. From the first century B.C., a popular tradition began to associate the magi specifically with dark arts and necromancy so that, in time, "magic" took on more negative connotations. So, although it seems clear that the magic arts go back all the way to ancient Mesopotamia and Egypt— and quite probably to that ancient rebel Nimrod, the father of god and goddess worship,[9] and his consort—for the purposes of this essay we will go back only as far as ancient Greece and Rome. It would be easy to dismiss witchcraft or the magic arts as having little to do with Western thought and culture, but the fact is that, from the beginning, the thought forms of Greek philosophy (a philosophy shaped deeply by Egyptian, Indian and Mesopotamian civilizations), with their politico-magical worldview, have fought against the biblical worldview and continue to do so today with vigour.

In the much-vaunted wisdom of the classical world, the philosopher Pythagoras (born around 570 B.C.) was a key Greek thinker who

---

[8]   Wyndham, "Gnostic Dualism and Medieval Witchcraft," 95.
[9]   See Alexander Hislop, *The Two Babylons* (New York: Loizeaux Brothers, 1943).

predated Plato by some 150 years. His life remains shrouded in occult myth. He came to be connected with the Persian magi in ancient literature, possibly as a pupil. Moreover, his doctrines involve a form of dualism and secret knowledge. He allegedly wrote of a trip he made to Hades, was credited with the power of bilocation (being in two places at once) and claimed he could remember four previous lives. His philosophic and religious debt to even more ancient occult doctrines and magic arts is clear. As ancient Greek historian Jacob Burckhardt has pointed out:

> The passage in Herodotus telling us that the so-called Orphics and followers of Bacchus were really Egyptian and Pythagoreans clearly shows that the Pythagorean and Egyptian creeds had somewhat similar elements just as the Orphic and Pythagorean rites were so similar as to be confused. We shall not try to establish whether he reached Babylon or not; there is no good reason to doubt that he did. He must have had some communication with India too, for his doctrine of metempsychosis is far more suggestive of India than of Egypt. The foremost legacy Pythagoras left to the Greeks was the new religion and system of ethics based on reincarnation and linked with asceticism.... Pythagoras founded a fellowship in order to propagate his hope of immortality. Like the Orphics he, too, regarded the body as a tomb or prison house of the spirit, which was of a higher, heavenly origin. We are not expressly told whether he taught that the spirit, after its transmigrations through many bodies, would achieve extinction as its reward, or whether, as Plato and Empedocles hoped, the spirit would be *absorbed into divinity*; its immortality, however, suggests that Pythagoras held the latter view.[10]

This is quite a remarkable set of details: that Greek culture and philosophy had some of their key thought forms shaped by Egyptian, Persian/Babylonian and Indian occult beliefs and magical arts. Moreover, that a form of magico-pantheism was basic to Greek philosophy.

---

[10] Jacob Burckhardt, *History of Greek Culture*, trans. Palmer Hilty (New York: Dover Publications, 2002), 283–284.

In fact, as Burckhardt goes on to argue, even in his mathematical teachings, Pythagoras mingled different categories together, so that he seems to have conceived of numbers as analogous to *forces* and number relations as analogous to *thoughts*. The "holy" numbers were 4 and 10, which led the adherent into the contemplation of the sublime. And when Pythagoras travelled to speak, reports tell us that he was announced as coming to the city not to teach, but to *heal*.[11] The conflation of science, magic and philosophy here is very telling. Much later, around the time of the preaching and healing of the apostles, a Pythagorean philosopher and alleged "wonder worker," Apollonius of Tyana (ca. A.D. 75), "was not only accused of killing a boy to divine the future of the Emperor Domitian, but his biographer, Philostratus, admits that the master was indeed an adept at necromancy."[12] The glory of Greece and Rome was not so glorious as some would like to pretend, and the popular notion that Greek thought liberated men from superstition and veneration of the gods is essentially myth.

The whole of Western philosophy has often been described as 'footnotes to Plato,' who was likewise interested in subterranean forces and occult power and is clearly indebted to Pythagoras. In his *Symposium*, Plato defines the demonic:

> "Everything that is daemonic", says Diotima to Socrates, "is intermediate between God and mortal. Interpreting and conveying the wishes of men to gods and the will of gods to men, it stands between the two and fills the gap.... God has no contact with man; only through the daemonic is there intercourse and conversation between men and gods, whether in the waking state or during sleep. And the man who is expert in such intercourse is a daemonic man, compared with whom the experts in arts or handicrafts are but journeymen."[13]

The person who could connect with the metaphysical world and its forces, bringing messages back and forth, was evidently highly

---

[11] Burckhardt, *History of Greek Culture*, 285–287.
[12] Wyndham, "Gnostic Dualism and Medieval Witchcraft," 96.
[13] Cited in E.R. Dodds, *Pagan and Christian in an Age of Anxiety* (1965, reprint; Cambridge: Cambridge University Press, 2000), 37.

regarded by Plato and his followers. It was not long before many pagans saw the gods of Greek culture as themselves daemons of an invisible and unknowable divinity. As Mark Wyndham has noted, "The rites which the Greeks and Romans associated with the arts of magic nearly always involved incantations directed at gods or daemons."[14] Superstitions, oracular dreams, the reading of entrails, spirit mediums, sexual rites with temple prostitutes, and potions for healing revealed in dreams by gods, fitted easily with various philosophic schools in the Greco-Roman world. Spirit mediums called up gods who were thought to be able to heal the sick and foretell the future, such that autonomous knowledge and power are clearly seen as the goals in man's effort to deal with his anxiety and build his civilization.

When, in the historically significant diary of Aristides (a contemporary of Marcus Aurelius), the author relates a dream in which he is confronted with his own statue and sees it change into a statue of Asclepius (god of divine healing), his interpretation of the dream is telling: "For Aristides, this dream is a symbol of his unity with his divine patron."[15] For the philosophers generally, the ultimate god was variously thought of as Aion, eternity, an abstraction, a pure unity, ultimate oneness—essentially a limiting concept, not the personal and holy God of the Bible. As Burckhardt explains, "With their doctrine that all is One and One is God, and with their definition of being, the Eleatics—Xenophanes, Parmenides and Zeno...were fledgling pantheists.... They sought to grasp the divine essence in its purity."[16]

At the foundations of the humanistic philosophical tradition in the West, therefore, are the basic tenets of the worldview of witchcraft: man is becoming a god and participates in divinity, and there are forces, powers and energies that can be accessed, granting power and knowledge to assist man on his quest for godhood.

SIMON PETER VERSUS SIMON MAGUS

One of the most fascinating accounts in the New Testament is the encounter between the apostle Peter and Simon Magus. The name

---

[14] Mark Wyndham, "Gnostic Dualism and the Origins of the Medieval Definition of Witchcraft," *The Journal of Christian Reconstruction: Symposium on Satanism*, vol. 1, no. 2 (Winter 1974): 93.

[15] Dodds, *Pagan and Christian*, 45.

[16] Burckhardt, *History of Greek Culture*, 289.

Magus indicates that this man was a sorcerer or magician. The early church regarded him as the archetypal heretic—indeed, as the father of Gnosticism within the philosophical dualistic tradition. In Acts 8, we learn of this Samaritan sorcerer, who thought he could acquire the power of the Holy Spirit with money to perform wonders:

A man named Simon had previously practiced sorcery in that city and astounded the Samaritan people, while claiming to be somebody great. They all paid attention to him, from the least of them to the greatest, and they said, "This man is called the Great Power of God!" They were attentive to him because he had astounded them with his sorceries for a long time. But when they believed Philip, as he preached the good news about the kingdom of God and the name of Jesus Christ, both men and women were baptized. Then even Simon himself believed. And after he was baptized, he went around constantly with Philip and was astounded as he observed the signs and great miracles that were being performed. When the apostles who were at Jerusalem heard that Samaria had welcomed God's message, they sent Peter and John to them.... Then Peter and John laid their hands on them, and they received the Holy Spirit. When Simon saw that the Holy Spirit was given through the laying on of the apostles' hands, he offered them money, saying, "Give me this power too, so that anyone I lay hands on may receive the Holy Spirit." But Peter told him, "May your silver be destroyed with you, because you thought the gift of God could be obtained with money! You have no part or share in this matter, because your heart is not right before God. Therefore repent of this wickedness of yours, and pray to the Lord that the intent of your heart may be forgiven you. For I see you are poisoned by bitterness and bound by iniquity" (Acts 8:9–23).

Magus' view of the work of the Spirit as a source of power that he might be able to buy indicates (as does his following Philip around) that he thought he might be tutored by the disciples, as though they were magical masters of a secret brotherhood who could teach him new techniques in witchcraft. Clearly the Pythagorean world-view—a desire to tap into secret knowledge and power—had a profound grip on him. The root of his desire for secret power and a new knowledge was not love for God, according to Peter, but rather bitterness and iniquity.

There is clear indication that a proto-Gnostic sect arose around Simon Magus, the influence of which was deeply felt in the early centuries of the church. The secret knowledge of early Gnostic cults was associated with magical arts, and once again the dream of godlike perfection that lifted humans above the laws of God was part of the worldview of witchcraft—an antinomianism that it seems Simon Magus taught. Clearly, he did not repent of his lawless actions, as Peter commanded him. According to the early church father Irenaeus, the mystic priests who belonged to Simon's sect, "lead profligate lives and practice magical arts. Being free, they live as they please."[17] For Simon and his disciples, lower angels or gods made the world, trying to hold men in bondage by moral laws; their goal was to be free of the laws of those lesser deities. So a Pythagorean dualism, demon invocation and profligate antinomianism were basic to his Gnostic teaching.

Libertinism and various forms of dualism have gone together ever since—what one does in the body is of no final consequence, because it is less than fully real. Distinctions at the level of created experience are temporary; the physical realm is less significant and real than the realm of spirit, ideas or ultimate reality, which is a pure unity where opposites are joined together and moral as well as creational distinctions disappear.

What is clear from Acts 8 is that, outside of Christ, man's religious quest is to be the "Great power of God"—to obtain a secret knowledge from the subterranean world and access power that will enable him to live as he pleases. It is equally clear that when this magician saw God at work through the apostles, he witnessed power of an altogether different quality. Magus was astounded at what God did through the disciples and so, in the grip of his iniquity, sought to acquire God's power for his own purposes. In this power encounter, the sorcery of men and devils is seen for the parody of the power of the living God that it is.

---

[17] Irenaeus, cited in Wyndham, "Gnostic Dualism and Medieval Witchcraft," 104.

MAGIC AND MODERNITY

The pagan, politico-magical worldview posited the king or emperor as high priest of a magical world order, connecting men with divinity via the demonic realm; as the Christian gospel spread and steadily overcame this worldview, the magical arts were increasingly abandoned, suppressed and forbidden. This, in itself, is something of a marvel—that the centuries-long established beliefs of Greece and Rome should give way, so rapidly, to Hebraic Christianity.

While Christianity was triumphant on the Western stage, this did not mean that the occult worldview vanished altogether. At the core of that ancient practice of witchcraft was the view that there can be no ultimate distinction between man and God, Creator and creature, their powers, persons and natures; instead, those worlds were collapsed and brought together.

In the Middle Ages, there were many manuscripts on astrology, professing to offer great secrets from antiquity and incorporating the work of alchemists, "whose tradition is as old as the earliest mining and metallurgical activities of men, whether in Greece, China or Africa."[18] This was not the quest for gold, but for the original matter, the Philosopher's Stone—the undifferentiated *prima materia* that could fuse the opposites of reality, a kind of heavenly substance that linked the divine and material realms. But it was the Renaissance that not only revived

> the memory and the monuments of Greece and Rome, it also rediscovered the pagan myths which used to shape the inner life of the Hellenistic and Roman citizens...whose origin goes back to prehistoric times and which took shape in Egypt, India, Mesopotamia and Iran.... Today we can safely assert that the Renaissance was the time when all these esoteric doctrines first presented themselves to Western man in the daylight of open speculation, that is, without efforts on the part of the church to suppress them. In this sense we may even say that the Renaissance is that period in Western intellectual history when the first serious attempt was conducted against the Christian con-

---

[18] Thomas Molnar, "The Gnostic Tradition and Renaissance Occultism," *The Journal of Christian Reconstruction: Symposium on Satanism*, vol. 1, no. 2 (Winter 1974): 113.

cept of God, men and creation.... Underneath the continued Aristotelianism of the universities, the occult systems had a relatively easy way of penetrating the intellectual circles of Renaissance Europe.[19]

What was understood as universal knowledge by the Renaissance scholar was thus a mastery of *occult arts*—only recently known in Christian lands. This was not simply knowledge, but the art of *manipulation*. There was, consequently, a widespread blending and mixing of the worldview of witchcraft with Hebrew and Christian thought during this period. In the sixteenth century, men like Caspar Schwenckfeld asserted, in very modern-sounding terms, that Christ is born in every man. As such, salvation is not necessary, but *theosis* (divinization) is the goal, since man and god are ultimately indistinguishable.[20] Magic arts simply facilitate this process.

The Reformation was in part a resistance to the Renaissance recovery of the worldview of witchcraft. It constituted the reaffirmation of biblical distinctions between Creator and creature, God's Word and man's ideas, and the regenerating power of the Holy Spirit and the manipulative occult arts. John Calvin attacked both judicial astrology and witchcraft in his *Avertissement contre l'astrologie judiciaire* in 1549.[21] He noted:

> Many incredible things are reported of Sorcerers. And truly when we hear them spoken of, we ought not only to dislike them, but also to be sorrowful in our hearts, yes, the very hairs of our heads ought to stand up when we encounter them. But we must also keep in mind that they are the vengeances of God upon such as have forsaken him.[22]

For Calvin, sorcery was a fact of every age and nation, due to the rejection of God's truth. Necromancy and other magic arts, to all

---

[19] Molnar, "The Gnostic Tradition," 122–114.

[20] See Molnar, "The Gnostic Tradition," 115.

[21] Allan Charles Kors and Edward Peters, ed., *Witchcraft in Europe, 400–1700: A Documentary History*, 2nd ed. (Philadelphia: University of Pennsylvania Press, 2001), 265.

[22] Calvin cited in Kors and Peters, ed., *Witchcraft*, 268.

appearance, seemed to be wonders where the living and the dead were brought together; but, for Calvin, "it is the devil that works such illusions."[23] Such magicians were not to be tolerated, but rather, "if Judges and Magistrates do their duties, it is certain that they will no more tolerate them than they tolerate murderers.... Why? It is an overthrowing of God's service and a perversion of the order of nature."[24]

The Reformation's resistance to the worldview of paganism was effective for a season, and the Christian church was greatly strengthened in the West in certain regions. But with the Enlightenment era came, once again, a blending of the pagan Greek mind with Christian thought forms.

The idealist philosophers conflated the individual mind and the cosmic mind, so that they saw the human mind as a particular manifestation of the cosmic mind—an idea inherited from the ancient Greeks. This concept led to what has been called Romantic biology, which saw nature and society as an organic whole. "The idea of nature as a realisation of the ultimate reality led to the belief in the unity of nature."[25] The ancient evolutionary concept of the basic kinship of all things spawned ideas like *recapitulation*, according to which the developmental history of the embryo supposedly paralleled the evolutionary history of the species; this idea has been shown to have influenced Charles Darwin.[26]

Romanticism joined the chorus singing nature's praise and insisted that human beings are simply part of this great organic whole— indeed, man was just the sum of all the lower beings—and so it affirmed the basic unity of everything. In this sense, some have argued that Romantic biology *re-enchanted* the world. But of course that re-enchantment was not with a renewed understanding of the providential Creator-God of Scripture, but rather with the subterranean powers. Human thought was integrating downward again into the void of "being" which it called "divine." If ever there were a case where men "put darkness for light and light for darkness" (Isaiah 5:20), this was it.

---

[23] Calvin cited in Kors and Peters, ed., *Witchcraft*, 269.
[24] Calvin cited in Kors and Peters, ed., *Witchcraft*, 270.
[25] Kenan Malik, *Man, Beast and Zombie: What Science Can and Cannot Tell Us About Human Nature* (London: Weidenfeld & Nicolson, 2000), 77.
[26] Malik, *Man, Beast and Zombie*, 77.

In the political and social realm, this meant the idealization of "primitive man," the "noble savage" of Rousseau and a belief in the revolutionary power of primitive acts and impulses as a source of renewal and self-realization. This, in turn, meant an exploration of the abnormal and, with it, the paranormal. Because all men need power, if we do not receive it from above, we will seek it from the created order below. Where God is replaced by chance or fate as the determining power over all things, meaning gives way to meaninglessness and the motive force for all things is no longer power from above, but primitive and regenerating power from below.

The significance of this for the faith and direction of society is far-reaching. Determinative power is then only chaotic and mindless. As such, when Sigmund Freud applied Darwinism to human psychology, he saw the three basic drives of man as hidden in the unconscious, a remnant of a primitive past; they were parricide, cannibalism and incest.[27] It is no surprise, then, that the modern Western world has seen "the rise of magic, witchcraft and occultism as means to the true source of power, and the revival of Satanism, power from below, as an article of faith and hope. In the post-Darwinian world, faith in Satan seems much more logical than faith in Jesus Christ."[28]

SOCIAL SORCERY AND POLITICAL WITCHCRAFT

In his poem "Satan Speaks," C.S. Lewis captures the essence of this modern, yet ancient faith:

I am Nature, the Mighty Mother,
I am the law: ye have none other.

I am the flower and the dewdrop fresh,
I am the lust in your itching flesh.[29]

The worldview of witchcraft seeks *knowledge* of correlations and correspondences rooted in a basic and original unity of everything

---

[27] See R.J. Rushdoony, *Freud* (Vallecito, CA: Ross House Books, 2006).

[28] R.J. Rushdoony, *The Death of Meaning* (Vallecito, CA: Ross House Books, 2002), 134.

[29] C.S. Lewis, *Poems* (Glasgow: Fount, 1994), 181.

(nature), so that man might find autonomous *power*—the unity and all-sufficiency of the self. Contrasts and distinctions, separations and divisions, keep the world in a place of struggle and conflict. Only when this oppositional reality ends, the world's agitation is over and multiplicity is reabsorbed into the One of Plotinus or Brahman, Atman or nirvana—when existence ceases—then alone can there be peace. Good and evil, right and wrong, truth and falsehood are all oppositional concepts that enslave man and society in conflict. Man must be reabsorbed into divinity—a pure unity—to find rest. But for that to take place, the *manliness of man* must be undone. Biblical multiplicity and distinctions must be eroded as illusions and man's idealized unity asserted at every point; the image of God must be defaced. In ancient magical arts, this was done through the orgy, cannibalism, demon invocation and perversion. Today, more sophisticated means are being added, while many of the others are still practiced.

For the Christian faith, the creation and government of all things is of God, and his power and wisdom that have created, defined and always govern all things transcends man, history and the universe. It is this that modern witchcraft is concerned to deny, as much as the magi of ancient Persia and the philosophers of Greece or India.

If we are to understand the radical changes in our society today as inspired by diabolic principalities and manifest in ideological strongholds that set themselves up against the knowledge of God (Ephesians 6:12; 2 Corinthians 10:4–6), then we must grasp the essential instrumentality of modern political life as engaged, wittingly or not, in *witchcraft*—employing a "secret" (elitist) knowledge in an attempt to join opposites. The goal of modern civil government has long ceased to be focused on the administration of justice. It is increasingly about the creation of a cosmic man who is divine, to join what God has separated and create a unified, distinction-free community that represents the end of all struggle. The purpose of such manipulation is *power*—the power to control and transform in terms of a revived *religious image of humanity*.

Our current culture is thus bent on defacing the image of God by denying that man is man and woman is woman, by negating the God-given nature of marriage and by politically manipulating people to believe and act as though an illusion were true—that homosexuality is normative, gender is fluid and that androgyny is the human ideal. Harvey has noted:

> Homosexuality and crossgender sexuality are embedded in witchcraft ritual, says Christopher Penczak in *Gay Witchcraft*. He notes that "Magick as a spiritual path is one filled with transgenderism. A magician of any sort must fluidly shift shapes between genders." Knowledge of both masculine and feminine aspects of oneself is the reason "why gays, lesbians, bisexuals and transgendered people were recognized as potentially talented in the mystical arts."[30]

None of this should surprise us, since, in the worldview of ancient pagan witchcraft, the original man was neither male nor female, but an androgynous figure possessing both sex characteristics. The hermaphrodite has always been important to pagan mythology, symbolizing the undifferentiated life force in which all conflicts are resolved—a sign and symbol for both perfection and chaos. We see the same idea in tantric symbols of Tibetan and Chinese origin.[31] "The Philosopher's Stone, the Original Man, the Androgyne and the sphere were expressions of totality, and as such, symbols of a finally abolished multiplicity, symbols of the whole and at the same time of Nothingness."[32] Further, the egalitarian political community is a kind of Philosopher's Stone on a large scale—the "original man" of vast, even global, proportions. Such an ideal, utopian city is in fact the "final symbol for man's divinization."[33]

The radical cultural confusion and irrationality of our time with regard to gender, marriage, sexuality and spirituality is not incidental, but basic to the revival of the worldview of witchcraft. Occultism is corrosive for every aspect of life and society. Each one seeks their own way, their own spiritual ascent by their own path and falls headlong into their own abyss. The erroneous hope is that political

---

30 Harvey, "Global Mainstreaming of Witchcraft," 55.
31 Molnar, "The Gnostic Tradition," 117.
32 Molnar, "The Gnostic Tradition," 117.
33 Molnar, "The Gnostic Tradition," 118.

formulas, utopias and egalitarian signs and symbols[34] will transition the inclusive, gender-fluid social order into a divine state. The problem for autonomous man is that sexuality is a fixed aspect of God's creation that proves a roadblock to man's desire to remake himself by his own magic words.

Of course, the pseudo-scientific manipulations don't end there. Great effort is being put into embryonic research and reproductive technologies, the goal of which is knowledge for the purposes of manipulation and the creation of a new man. Many strains of witchcraft in times past abhorred pregnancy accidentally produced from their perversions and orgiastic rituals and so would abort the fetus, then to be cut up and eaten by members of the order. In our own time, we have the mass slaughter of unborn babies on a scale well beyond that imagined in earlier societies. We have widespread promiscuity, the abhorrence of reproduction and the sale of babies' body parts, by government-funded organisations like Planned Parenthood, on a black market for all manner of "research."

These practices all stem from the worldview not of *science*, but of *witchcraft*. An autonomous realm of knowledge is sought for the acquisition of lawless power, so that man might become a god. Social sorcery is all around us. The modern Simon Magus believes that he has solved the riddle of existence, like Pythagoras of old, and that he "has changed the universe into what he wanted it to be (abolition of good and evil, fusion of opposites etc.), he gained a supra-rational power, a vantage point where he usurps the right of deciding the real and the unreal, being and non-being."[35] Such is the point our society has arrived at today. And, on such a basis, politicians, judges and cultural elites make their rulings on marriage and sexuality and publish their curricula. Like the father of Gnosticism, they are poisoned by bitterness and bound by iniquity (Acts 8:23), though they walk in ignorance.

In the face of all this sophisticated occult power, the Christian cannot flinch or falter. Autonomous knowledge and power are dis-

---

[34] See Rainbow Health Ontario (www.RainbowHealthOntario.ca) and PFLAG Canada (www.pflagcanada.ca) for illustrations of signs and symbols and magic words that are meant to manipulate people into the image of the androgyne.

[35] Molnar, "The Gnostic Tradition," 119.

integrating because they are satanic illusions. Satan can lie, deceive, manipulate, steal, kill and seek to destroy, but he can do nothing constructive. He cannot remake man or the world, and his path is one only of death, not of life. And so, the worldview of witchcraft, though it has been resuscitated for a season, has no more of a future than it had when Simon Peter confronted Simon Magus with the gospel of power—God's power.

This world is God's creation and moves only in terms of *his* will and purpose. His Word cannot be broken and no one can stay his hand. In Jesus Christ are hid all the treasures of wisdom and knowledge, and he is both the power and the wisdom of God (Colossians 2:3). Christ instructed his disciples to wait in Jerusalem, telling them, "You will receive power when the Holy Spirit has come on you and you will be my witnesses" (Acts 1:8). This is the only source of true and integrating power. And the gospel still has the power to change the world, because it carries with it the regenerating power of the Holy Spirit. We are given this unshakeable assurance that, whatever the machinations of darkness may be, "The God of peace will soon crush Satan under your feet" (Romans 16:20).

4

THE ACCOMMODATION MOTIVE: HOW MANY KINGDOMS?

"Your Kingdom come, your will be done, on earth as it is in Heaven" (Matthew 6:10).

We have examined some of the key problems with Western culture, grounded in the reality that, as a society, we have turned away from God and his Word, exchanging true worship for the idol of self. We now come to perhaps the most prominent way in which the church has attempted to answer the question of how the Christian should live in the contemporary context. This chapter is a consideration of what has been dubbed "Two Kingdoms" theology and, specifically, its implications for culture. Discussing this theological perspective is, for most people, like walking into a foggy room where you can't quite find your feet and are not entirely sure where the furniture is. This is because, especially in recent years, various doctrinal streams— some mutually exclusive—have used the term "Two Kingdoms" to describe their theology. The task of analysis is made quite difficult, due to the sheer quantity of the popular literature generated, with different emphases, and the regular *equivocation* with terms like *kingdom, church, sphere, age* and *realm* that the Two Kingdoms (henceforth, 2K) advocates tend to engage in, especially when making an effort to recommend their view to a more historically Reformed and covenant-literate audience.

Brian Mattson, a cultural theologian and colleague of mine at the Center for Cultural Leadership in California, has offered a helpful summary of the basic tenets of 2K theology, as set out by its leading contemporary thinker, David VanDrunen:

> The central dogma is that while God rules over and governs the entire world, he does so in two distinct ways. His rule is divided into two distinct realms, each with its own origin, its own norms, and its own destiny. The one realm has its origin in creation (recapitulated in the covenant with Noah) and is governed by God's general providence, its norms are provided by natural law or general revelation, and its destiny is strictly temporal--that is, it is destined to pass away. This realm they call the "common" or "civil" kingdom. It is made up of believers and unbelievers alike, and it encompasses all activities that are legitimately engaged in by everyone. This is the realm, in other words, common to all humanity. It includes things like civil government, marriage and family, the economic marketplace, arts, education, and, no doubt, much more. The other realm, by way of contrast, has its origin in the new creation inaugurated by Christ and is governed by God's special grace in the gospel, its norms are provided by God's special revelation in the Bible, and its destiny is eternal. This realm they call the "special" or "redemptive" kingdom. It is made up strictly of believers, and it is found exclusively in the church of Jesus Christ. So, for example, only Christians take the Lord's Supper, but all sorts of people vote for public officials. Therefore, the Lord's Supper belongs to the "redemptive" kingdom and voting belongs to the "common" kingdom. The crucial point is that while individual Christians actually inhabit both of these realms (VanDrunen's

latest book is entitled, *Living In God's Two Kingdoms*), the realms themselves (and all that they entail) do not overlap.[1]

While the exact content and contours of the 2K view can appear hazy, even after a clear definition like that, it is nonetheless the case that those who have tracked in some measure with the debate are likely familiar with well-circulated, catchy one-liners from David VanDrunen and Michael Horton like, "There is no Christian way to change a diaper" or "There is no such thing as Christian stir fry." These somewhat sardonic quips seem obviously true, until you observe that the cogency of these *defeater* arguments (i.e. allegedly demonstrating that there is no distinctly Christian view of most of life) rely on the hearer not giving them careful thought. For example, in Islam, *Shari'ah* law does actually govern how you go to the toilet; there is an Islamic way to use the washroom. The Greek cynics thought nothing of defecating in public to show their contempt for propriety. Or, regarding the possibility of a "Christian" stir fry, this would depend on whether in fact you were a seventeenth or eighteenth-century cannibal (like the Carib Indians, of which the term *cannibal* is a corruption), who periodically enjoyed stir-fried man-flesh, or a Jewish or Muslim individual observing religious food preparation laws. Indeed, there are many Christians who take biblical dietary laws seriously (as Jesus himself did) and would not stir fry pork or rodents, dog, cat or any unclean animal—including those popular sea creatures, eaten in vast quantities today, that feed on the bottom of the ocean. In short, issues of hygiene and ablutions, or questions of food preparation, are not as obviously "non-religious" as they first appear when hearing these populist and superficial arguments; there are, in fact, Christian and non-Christian ways to engage in all these activities. As the Christian thinker Evan Runner rightly noted, all of life is religion:

Thus we arrive at the insight that our *whole life is religion*. And that not only for Christian believers (true religion), but also for

---

[1]   Brian Mattson, "Cultural Amnesia: What Makes Pietism Possible" (lecture, CCL Annual Conference, San Francisco, CA, October 2011); http://drbrianmattson.com/ccl-lectures-2011/; accessed May 2016.

unbelievers. For unbelief is not described in Scripture as absence of belief, but as mis-directed belief. Religion…is man's ineradicable situation: he has been created "before God" (*coram Deo*) and must render an account of his doings and ways. It is the role of the Word that comes from God to illumine our hearts and direct our goings. But likewise, men who lack this light and direction are prompted, by reason of their (now perverted) religious nature to do for themselves what the word of God ought to do for them…fallen man, being a religious being (who must have a word that reveals the order and structure of things), never just 'accepts the facts' but rather invents, finds a way to put the facts so that he will be safe without God. In this way, apostate man appropriates to his own heathen pistical phantasy the role that the word of God really has, and thus from the beginning places himself in a world where the relations are (imagined) other than they really are. He lives the lie. Human analysis takes place within the context of the lie or of the truth.[2]

This scriptural clarity is missing in the 2K arguments, because it appears that their primary concern is to deny just that—that all of life is religious. Instead, vast swathes of life are *neutral* or *common*. Hence, no distinctly Christian methods for thinking about cooking or ablutions or family!

EXAMINING BEDROCK BELIEFS

Given the ambiguities and confusion inherent in the presentation of 2K thought, how might we begin to uncover the core convictions of the 2K thinkers? Dr. Matthew Tuininga, a leading 2K advocate and popularizer, has in the recent past affirmed that David VanDrunen is the foremost contemporary 2K theorist, especially as VanDrunen elaborates this view in his more programmatic statement, *Living in God's Two Kingdoms*.[3] This book Tuininga has historically seen as effectively the gold standard of the contemporary effort to set out the

---

[2] Evan Runner, *Walking in the Way of the Word: The Collected Writings of H. Evan Runner* (Grand Rapids: Paideia Press, 2009), 180–181.

[3] See Matthew Tuininga: https://matthewtuininga.wordpress.com/tag/david-van-drunen/; accessed August 19, 2016.

2K view, so, for the purposes of this article, I will take VanDrunen's presentation of 2K thought in *Living in God's Two Kingdoms* as normative and the clearest expression of what I think has, with some justice, been dubbed the *Escondido* theology.[4] It will be helpful to begin with a few general remarks, to set the broader context for this important debate, and then proceed to highlight what I consider to be three essential problems with 2K theology, which severely undermine the Christian's engagement with contemporary culture.

By way of prologue, then, it is important to say there can be little question that there are real elements of novelty in this theology that seeks to represent itself as Reformed. The contemporary 2K proponents have stirred controversy in Reformed circles, because it is not really plausible to view 2K thinking as simply a variation on a Reformed theme, which makes little or no difference in regard to the gospel's engagement with culture.[5] Indeed, the provenance of this

---

[4] Based on my experience in a recent debate with Matthew Tuininga, it seems that he may be seeking to distance himself from David VanDrunen (as well as Darryl Hart and Michael Horton) and position himself as one occupying a middle ground between VanDrunen and the Kuyperian perspective. Debate reviewers are divided as to whether this stance represents a substantive theological difference or is merely a pragmatic strategy for the purpose of seeking to make 2K theology more palatable to a Dutch Reformed audience. In my debate with Tuininga, to my surprise and that of the audience, he carefully avoided any effort to defend VanDrunen's radical 2K view—including the lynch-pin of VanDrunen's argument for a "common kingdom," based on God's covenant with Noah. Instead, Tuininga offered up his own interpretation of Calvin that suggested yet another 2K variation or permutation, this time dividing up earthly institutions in terms of the eschatological "age" to which they belong (rather than utilizing VanDrunen's theological constructs of common and redemptive kingdoms). Here the dichotomy is drawn (and I think radically overdrawn) between the present age and the age to come. Although his exact position was unclear and not well formed (or at least not well articulated) with respect to the relationship of God's kingdom to that of the culture at large, presumably those institutions that are seen as simply part of the "present age" are not obligated to be distinctly Christian. Here, the Kingdom of God is largely postponed to the age to come, except in so far as it is manifest in the church. I could find little difference between what Dr. Tuininga was arguing and the position of many premillennials and dispensationalists. I nonetheless detected indications that Tuininga was uncomfortable with some of the more radical assertions of the leading 2K advocates. See http://www.ezrainstitute.ca/resource-library/debates/two-kingdoms-and-cultural-obedience.

[5] John Frame's series of book reviews in *The Escondido Theology* (Lakeland, FL: Whitefield Media Productions, 2011) makes it very plain that there are real elements of novelty here that have not traditionally been seen as Reformed distinctives. There

ecclesiasticization of the gospel is especially noteworthy. It appears to have a clear lineage, coming to us as a variation of the scholastic nature-grace dualism of Roman Catholic theology, offering a similar two-storey view of reality, though one that has been "Protestantized" by VanDrunen. VanDrunen, in fact, graduated from Loyola, a private Catholic university in Chicago, where, it seems plausible to suggest, he became enamoured with the thought of Thomas Aquinas and was doubtless immersed in the Catholic nature-grace distinction and natural law theory—indeed, he has become a fierce apologist for "natural law" thinking.[6] It seems to me that he has attempted to marry a theologically dualistic perspective, inherited from Greek philosophy, with the covenantal-kingdom view of Reformed thought.

Second, and critically, VanDrunen has openly rejected the unified plotline of *Creation-Fall-Redemption* as a total world and life-view for Christian thinking as an invention of the Dutch philosopher Herman Dooyeweerd. Along with this, he has rejected the very idea of a Christian *worldview* as simply borrowed from German idealism. He stated, "A Christian answer to every question? There isn't one. There are a range of answers on how to use specific things in the world."[7] VanDrunen's idea that there is not a covenant-keeping (specifically Christian) and covenant-breaking (non-believing) answer or direction to every matter of life points to the throbbing heart of this debate. Whether or not we use the term *worldview* (or supplant it with another word) to describe the *scriptural perspective* on reality is irrelevant to the question of whether God's work in creation and history is bifurcated into two realms—a "common kingdom" and a "redemptive kingdom." Indeed, such a radical bifurcation is no less a *worldview* than Abraham Kuyper's neo-Calvinism. The 2K advocates tell us that the first realm, the common kingdom, is governed by *natural law* (an originally Stoic concept filled with difficulties, the *actual content* of which nobody seems to grasp with any clarity) and

---

are, however, strong Lutheran and scholastic themes present—hence the label "Escondido" theology, given that several of its major exponents have emerged from Westminster Seminary in Escondido California.

    [6] See David VanDrunen, *Natural Law and the Two Kingdoms: A Study in the Development of Reformed Social Thought* (Grand Rapids: Eerdmans, 2009).

    [7] David VanDrunen, "How Many Kingdoms?" *Christian Renewal: Two Kingdoms, Two Views* 34, no. 4 (November 18, 2015): 14.

the second kingdom by God's special revelation, so that Christians must live life playing *musical chairs* between a common and a redemptive kingdom—and it is often unclear which one you are standing in at any given moment.

Thirdly, it should be noted that the focus of much of the 2K debate has been in the realm of historical theology (which theologians too often confuse with Scripture), with regard to what Augustine, Calvin and Luther meant exactly by their use of the terms *kingdom* or *two kingdoms*. There is no doubt that this is an interesting area of inquiry. Answering that question is not the concern of this article, but it is troubling that VanDrunen's defense of his natural law perspective, which is important to his 2K thought, is almost devoid of Scripture, the majority of the argument centring on his controversial conclusions about what Luther and Calvin are supposed to have meant by the terminology.[8]

Whatever the truth about the diverse and nuanced views of the various Reformers and their forebears, an historical controversy cannot be allowed to *determine* how we relate the gospel to culture today. For my own part, it seems to me that what Calvin was very much concerned with in referencing *two kingdoms*, writing as he was in the midst of old *Christendom*, was not an approximation of visible church and state, but the contrast between the *invisible*, or spiritual, and *visible*, temporal kingdoms. His contrasting, spiritual kingdom life is not over against Christian vocation in human culture (that would contradict his doctrine of vocation, and the very project of Geneva), but is over against the visible, Roman Magisterium, with its vast, sacerdotal, institutional structures. It seems to me that, for Calvin, the truly invisible and spiritual must reform the visible and temporal, and all laymen are priests in this task! Calvin occupied an essentially Christianized culture and was, throughout his career, facing down a corrupted church! Calvin must be read in light of the

---

[8] See David VanDrunen, *Natural Law and the Two Kingdoms*. VanDrunen has elsewhere attempted to demonstrate a biblical basis for natural law: David VanDrunen, *A Biblical Case for Natural Law* (Grand Rapids: Acton Institute, 2006). I believe that there are real shortcomings in this effort, and can do no better than to point to John Frame's critique, "Review of David Van Drunen's *A Biblical Case for Natural Law*," Frame-Poythress, May 10 2012; http://frame-poythress.org/review-of-david-van-drunens-a-biblical-case-for-natural-law/.

conflict in his own day, not hijacked for the peculiar purpose of show-ing why twenty-first century Christians should let the "common kingdom" (family, state, culture) go its own way without special revelation—a view it seems incredible to assign to Calvin. If the 2K proponents are right about Calvin, then Calvin's own disciples, like John Knox, radically misinterpreted and misapplied him cultur-ally, and the Puritans, his immediate English heirs, simply got him all wrong.

Fourthly, it should also be noted that, sociologically, this culturally retreatist theology is emanating from the comfortable academic halls of white, middle-class, Christian enclaves like Escondido and Grand Rapids—not from the fires of persecution in the churches of Syria or Pakistan. I do not believe it is viable to take 2K theology seriously in areas of the world where Christians are suffering, sometimes terribly, in lands dominated by false religions. It is all too easy to speak of a "common kingdom" governed by norms we can all agree upon from comfortable academic chairs within a culture that has been deeply transformed by the gospel for centuries. But what can really be said of the notion of a "common kingdom" governed by "natural law" that all essentially agree upon, in places where Christians are being beheaded and raped, or their children murdered in front of them?

Fifthly, I am convinced that the reason for the growing popularity of the 2K theology is not its biblical or apologetic cogency, but its timely provision of a *convenient exit* from the growing confrontation of God's kingdom truth with an apostate Western culture that is determined to violate God's norms and despoil the image of God in man at every turn. It provides an alternative to the antithesis for-mulated by Abraham Kuyper and the challenge that God's law brings against our rebellious order. Many of the Arminian funda-mentalists in the United States dream of *historical* escape from creation with Jerry Jenkins and Tim Lahaye via the secret rapture, and now some in Reformed circles hope to *theologically* abandon creation to Satan under the pretext that God is not redeeming *this creation*, so it can go its "common way." I believe both of these escapist views are wrong, and, if we have any hope of addressing the challenges facing us in the West today, we cannot allow a doctrine of retreat or escape to rule the church. God nowhere commands commonality, but only obedience.

In short, it is my contention that the Bible knows nothing of a common and a redemptive kingdom, but only of God's kingdom and Satan's kingdom; of covenant keepers and breakers; of the kingdom of darkness and the kingdom of light (1 Peter 2:9). The only thing the inhabitants of these spiritual kingdoms of light and darkness have in common is that we all live as creatures of God, under his total providence, in his creation, under the blessings or curses of the covenant that the triune God established from the beginning. The non-believer simply lives as an "outlaw" on God's earth and as a rebel to his kingdom, formally denying, but at the same time always supported and sustained by, the reality of God's Word-revelation. The non-believer thus lives on *borrowed capital* from, but not in a common kingdom with believers. The Christian lives thetically; the non-believer, antithetically. As Paul writes in 2 Corinthians 6:14–16, "Do not be unequally yoked with unbelievers. For what partnership has righteousness with lawlessness? Or what fellowship has light with darkness? What accord has Christ with Belial? Or what portion does a believer share with an unbeliever? What agreement has the temple of God with idols?"

In examining the 2K teaching, I detect three central problems:

1. The *philosophical* problem
2. The *theological* problem
3. The *sociological* or *cultural* problem

THE PHILOSOPHICAL PROBLEM
The Reformed theologian Herman Bavinck brilliantly identified an age-old, essentially philosophic problem that has dogged the church from its beginnings, during the decline of the Greco-Roman world:

At the bottom of every serious question lies the self-same problem: The relation of faith and knowledge, of theology and philosophy, of authority and reason, of head and heart, of Christianity and humanity, of religion and culture, of heavenly and earthly vocation, of religion and morality, of the contemplative and the active life, of Sabbath and workday, of church and state—all these and many other questions are determined by the problem of the relation between creation and recreation, between the work of the Father and the work of the Son. Even the simple, common man finds himself caught up in this struggle whenever he senses the tension that exists between his earthly and heavenly calling.[9]

The question of the relation between *creation* and *re-creation* is at the heart of the problem with 2K theology, because it deals with their relationship on the basis of an unscriptural philosophy. The result is the introduction into Reformed thought of the fundamental antinomies Bavinck mentions. *What is that unscriptural philosophy?*

The 2K theological paradigm is implicitly governed by a faulty philosophical assumption of *duality* that is clearly influenced by Greek thought. The roots of this idea are found in Plato—though it was Aristotle who first coined the term *form-matter*. Herman Dooyeweerd notes that

> the "form-matter" ground-motive controlled Greek thought and civilization from the beginning of the Greek city states. It originated in the unreconciled conflict within Greek religious consciousness between the ground-motive of the ancient nature religions and the ground motive of the then more recent culture religion—the religion of the Olympian deities.[10]

The dichotomy between the realm of eternal ideas or *ideals* on the one hand, and the ordinary *material realm* on the other, was seen as the basic distinction within nature. The Gnostics and Neo-Platonists later held this dichotomy to be between the "spiritual" and "material." There have been other ways of dividing up reality dualistically, of course. But it is important to notice that these realms are not different *perspectives* on the same unified reality; they constitute dual ontological realms within a broader whole—they were both thought to have real existence. This basic philosophical division in its various permutations soon came to be viewed in terms of a hierarchy; one

---

9 Herman Bavinck, "Common Grace," trans. Raymond C. Van Leeuwen, *Calvin Theological Journal* 24, no. 1 (1989): 35–65, 55–56.

10 Herman Dooyeweerd, *Roots of Western Culture: Pagan, Secular and Christian Options—Collected Works*, Series B, vol. 15, ed. D.F.M. Strauss (Grand Rapids: Paideia Press, 2012), 16.

realm is higher—an upper storey that is more important—and one realm is lower, a lower storey that is considered less important. The subsequent Roman Catholic formulation of this duality was nature versus grace, where the upper storey of grace supplemented and elevated the lower storey of nature. This was an attempted synthesis of the Christian doctrine of grace with the Greek idea of nature.

As reformulated by modern 2K theology, the higher storey is the spiritual *realm of redemption* in Christ—most important and eternal —and the lower storey is the *realm of creation* and *common culture*— less important and only transitory or temporary. It's not that we charge them with conceiving of nature as incomplete in the essentially Roman Catholic sense, but rather, holding that creation (the common kingdom) has no direct relationship with grace at all. These realms, for the most part, are kept strictly distinct. This, it seems, is the main objective of 2K theology—to separate creation and redemption. Grace is good in its place, but it must stay there. To put it another way, nature (or creation) and grace run on parallel tracks that never effectually meet, and, as a result, God's redemptive realm is not redeeming this creation or culture—they are, to all intents and purposes, separate *ontic* spheres.

If all the 2K advocates were saying is that church and state are two distinct jurisdictions or spheres under God, or that there is both a kingdom of darkness and kingdom of light, governed by opposing principles, or that the present age is not identical in character, finality and glory with the consummation age, we would not have a controversy. But 2K theology seems to be arguing that there are two distinct realms, characterized by distinct laws and norms *that do not intersect.* There is a fundamental cleavage that cannot be bridged between creation and redemption; between this age and the age to come; between law and gospel; between nature and grace; between the church and the culture. Scripture, however, plainly indicates that there is only *one unified creation, visible and invisible* (Colossians 1:15–17), made by the triune God from the beginning, and that its life, civilization and culture must be considered simply in terms of two different *ethical* or religious positions—in Christ or outside of Christ; covenant-abiding or covenant-violating; the regenerate in heart and the unregenerate. Thus, the antitheses of 2K thought are imaginary, simply because God's world and work are artificially divided.

Brian Mattson, in his excellent work on Herman Bavinck, shows us Bavinck's solution to the problem. We cannot view God's *redemptive grace* as somehow discontinuous with (or juxtaposed to) the original creation, or unrelated to God's original purpose. If 2K *dualism* is right, then Christ's work of redemption is not directly related to the Father's work of creation through the Son, which would divide God against himself. That is to say, if a common creational kingdom exists parallel to a redemptive kingdom with unrelated purposes, then God himself has an identity crisis—and if God does, so shall we! A faulty philosophy here results in all manner of false dichotomies between sacred and secular, nature and grace, gospel and culture, and thereby hopelessly bifurcates our existence.[11]

In short, all false dualisms divide peoples' lives in the *wrong place*, in violation of Scripture. This is significant, because it results in a failure to see the true dividing line in history—the *heart* of man. The book of Proverbs says, "Out of the heart spring the issues of life" (Proverbs 4:23). In like manner, Jesus tells us that "out of the abundance of the heart, the mouth speaks" (Matthew 12:24). Scripture calls us to love God with all our heart—that is, from the core of our being—as the most basic commandment (Matthew 22:37). And Paul tells us that God's judgement will disclose the "purposes of the heart" (1 Corinthians 4:5). The renewed heart and the rebellious heart are the two essential conditions of man and categorically define the kingdoms of darkness and light. It is for this reason that Jesus made plain that "the Kingdom of God is within you" (Luke 17:21). We simply cannot point, with the 2K proponents, to the visible church and say, "Look, there's the kingdom of God," since the kingdom of God starts in the heart of man. Biblically, wherever Christ reigns in a person's life (family, home, church, state, etc.), there his kingdom reign is. As our hearts and lives are transformed, the Holy Spirit redirects *every activity* so that, at the root of our being, God's redemptive work begins to change everything—not simply the church. In fact, when *World Magazine* and *Christianity Today* tell us that 57% of

---

[11] Brian Mattson, "Grace Restores and Perfects Nature: Herman Bavinck and 21st Century Cultural Transformation" (lecture, CCL Annual Conference, San Francisco, CA, October 2011); http://drbrianmattson.com/ccl-lectures-2011/; accessed May 2016. My thanks to Dr. Brian Mattson for the use of this outstanding paper. I am indebted to his research in this monograph.

pastors in America are regularly wrestling with pornography and 5% would say they were addicted to hard-core pornography,[12] can we really say of those church situations, "Look, the kingdom of God, manifest in the institution of the church"? The line of demarcation runs through the heart, not an institution.

The fact that it is not ontological dualism, but the regeneration of the heart that divides history and culture clearly rules out the possibility of VanDrunen's idea of a *common kingdom*. He has argued in his book, *Living in God's Two Kingdoms*, that Christ's resurrection and ascension, and the establishment of the church have "not changed the truths of calculus or the way water flows [or the]...objective obligations [of] a plumber."[13] With this we can formally agree, but not as a justification for the dualistic idea of a common kingdom distinct from the redemptive. Here VanDrunen and the 2K advocates confuse *structure* with *direction* in creation. Satan could not alter the laws and norms of God's creation at the Fall—creation always has and always will serve and obey Christ. Of course, we do not do anything as stupid as deny that this *structure* (the way water flows, for example) holds true for the believer and the unbeliever, whether they obey God or not. A physical law simply describes what *is*, and moral laws and norms describe what *ought* to be.

It is therefore man's rebellion against God's Word-revelation in creation and in Scripture that places him in the kingdom of darkness in his vocation, marriage, school and every other sphere. His rebellious mind and heart affect every aspect of his life and thinking. The covenant-breaker needs to be regenerated, redeemed and his thoughts taken captive to obey Christ in every area of life. This restoration we call *redemption*, and the whole driving force of this reality, scripturally, is that God is *maintaining* his original purposes for creation. This redemption is so central to God's plan that he sent his Son, Jesus Christ, to die to bring it about. This Jesus Christ is both the *image of the invisible God* and the *second Adam* (Colossians 1:15;

---

[12] See Hazel Torres, "57% Percent of Pastors, 64% of Youth Pastors in U.S. Struggle with Porn Addiction, Survey Shows," *Christianity Today*, January 30 2016; http://www. christiantoday.com/article/57.percent.of.pastors.and.64.of.youth.pastors.in.u.s. struggle.with.porn.addiction.survey.shows/78178.htm; accessed August 19, 2016.

[13] David VanDrunen, *Living in God's Two Kingdoms: A Biblical Vision for Christianity and Culture* (Wheaton: Crossway, 2010), 170.

1 Corinthians 15:45). Both of these terms are used to describe Christ in the New Testament, because his work directly connects God's original creation of Adam with the image of God. Grace, therefore, restores and perfects creation and brings God's original purposes to fulfilment through the gospel. In other words, grace is organically related to creation, and re-creation is inseparable from creation—they are not two distinct realities, as the 2K advocates would have it.

The seriousness of the philosophical error of historical and *ontological dualism* culminates in VanDrunen's very dubious handling of Romans 8:19–24. Here, Paul tells us that all creation is longing for the resurrection of our bodies, having been subjected to frustration, in the hope of creation being liberated into the glorious freedom of the children of God. So Paul argues that the liberation of creation from futility is bound to the physical resurrection of man—that is, Christ's redemptive work has inescapable and decisive implications for *all creation*. But VanDrunen brings his philosophical dualism to bear in his interpretive effort. For him, this creation wasn't meant to last forever. Re-creation is, therefore, set out as a completely distinct realm. The radical nature of his controlling ground-motive of nature-grace, common kingdom-redemptive kingdom dualism makes him interpret Paul's liberation of creation as "giving way" or yielding to the new creation. As Mattson points out, VanDrunen thinks this creation longs to be euthanized[14]—to have a good death. This creation will supposedly give place to the new creation, and this is precisely why, when it comes to questions of gospel and culture, Christianity and the state, God's law and the legislature, the two kingdoms don't mix. We cannot transform the old creation with the power of the new creation, for the old is going to die. The elements of grace thus belong only in the church—a non-temporal and *super*-natural institution.

This view is highly problematic, because it throws into doubt the reality and purpose of the incarnation of Christ and, specifically, the doctrine of the resurrection of the body. If there were no clear doctrine of the resurrection, there would be no basis for continuity at all between the two realms. It appears that VanDrunen is at least sensitive to this problem, and so he recovers his Christianity at the

---

[14] Mattson, "Grace Restores and Perfects Nature."

last by saying, "our earthly bodies are the only part of the present world that scripture says will be transformed and taken up into the world to come."[15] Mattson in astonishment writes, "This from a text where Paul just emphasized the groaning and longing of the *whole creation* for liberation!"[16] The biblical gospel doesn't just resurrect and redeem bodies, but minds, hearts, relationships, souls and our work—indeed all our cultural fruits. Contrary to VanDrunen and Matthew Tuininga, we don't merely "witness" God's kingdom established (at the end of time), we work and pray for it now as fellow-workers and co-labourers with God (1 Corinthians 3:9). Jesus taught us to pray, "Thy Kingdom come, thy will be done, *on earth*, as it is in heaven." We might ask the 2K proponents which kingdom he was referring to, and if it is of another age or indeed of another creation altogether, why would we pray for it to come on earth now? In fact, Scripture is abundantly clear that it is not just our bodies, but also our works that go with us into eternity:

> For we are God's *fellow workers*. You are God's field, God's building. According to the grace of God given to me, like a skilled master builder I laid a foundation, and someone else is building upon it. Let each one take care how he builds upon it. For no one can lay a foundation other than that which is laid, which is Jesus Christ. Now if anyone builds on the foundation with gold, silver, precious stones, wood, hay, straw – each one's work will become manifest, for the Day will disclose it, because it will be revealed by fire, and the fire will test what sort of work each one has done. If the work that anyone has built on the foundation *survives*, he will receive a reward. If anyone's work is burned up, he will suffer loss, though he himself will be saved, but only as through fire. Do you not know that you are God's temple and that God's Spirit dwells in you? (1 Corinthians 3:9–16)

Over against the radical dualism of 2K theology, Bavinck summed up the Reformed perspective beautifully when he said, "Christianity…

---

[15] VanDrunen, *Living in God's Two Kingdoms*, 66.
[16] Mattson, "Grace Restores and Perfects Nature."

creates no new cosmos, but rather makes the cosmos new."[17] In Christ, we are already a new creation (2 Corinthians 5:17). By his Spirit and through his people, God is reconciling all things to himself in heaven and earth (Colossians 1:20). We are privileged participants in God's cosmic redemption.

THE THEOLOGICAL PROBLEM

We have seen that, in 2K theology, the civic or *common kingdom* and *redemptive kingdom* (as realms), with their own origins, norms and destinies, barely overlap; they are not organically related, yet the Christian must live in both in terms of a *functional dualism*. Of course, as Christians, scholars like VanDrunen, Horton and Tuininga do not believe themselves dependent on a philosophical dualism to support their *common kingdom* and *redemptive kingdom* bifurcation—the first said to be rooted in creation, the latter in re-creation. The norms of the common kingdom—allegedly universally accessible moral principles—are distinct from the laws and norms of the redemptive kingdom, which are founded upon special revelation.

The central motive of the theological arguments for 2K theology seems to be releasing the common or civil kingdom from any obligation to obedience to God's special revelation. VanDrunen argues, "in a certain sense, Scripture is not the appropriate moral standard for the civil kingdom."[18] This is a staggering statement, and very difficult to square with historic Reformed thought. It implies that outside the church, the moral standards of Scripture don't fully apply. Why is Scripture not appropriate for the common kingdom? According to VanDrunen:

Biblical morality is characterized by an indicative-imperative structure. That is, all of its imperatives (moral commands) are preceded by and grounded in indicatives (statements of fact), either explicitly or implicitly. The most important indicative that grounds the imperatives in scripture is that the recipients of scripture are the covenant people, that is, members of the community of the covenant of grace.[19]

---

[17] Bavinck, *Common Grace*, 27.
[18] VanDrunen, *A Biblical Case for Natural Law*, 38.
[19] VanDrunen, *A Biblical Case for Natural Law*, 39.

By subtle theological sleight-of-hand, we are essentially told that the civic or *common kingdom* contains many non-believers (as well as believers) and, since Scripture is given to the *redemptive kingdom* people and not to non-believers, the Bible cannot apply directly to the common kingdom. Remarkable! Quite why God has Amos prophesy to the pagan nations around Israel in terms of God's covenant-law standards, or sends Jonah to the heart of the Assyrian empire to call them to national repentance and faith, or uses Daniel and his friends to bring the king of Babylon to acknowledge the covenantal God of Israel as having total dominion, becomes a mystery.

Clearly, the ultimate grounds for ethical conduct in Scripture is not a redemptive covenant relationship, but the character of God, and man as his image-bearer. Moreover, God established creational ordinances before the Fall with our first parents, which clearly included cultural labour, Sabbath rest and marriage—these govern and bind all men, irrespective of their covenantal status. As John Frame has pointed out, "The whole Bible…is God's standard for all people, believers and unbelievers alike. God has not ordained separate ethics for believers and unbelievers."[20] VanDrunen's ill-conceived attempt to find a non-religious civil morality appears to lie at the heart of his theological constructs. He needs his scholastic doctrine of a non-religious natural law to create a common kingdom. It is as though the theological project is worked out after the fact. The 2K theorists begin with philosophically dualistic assumptions (that we have considered), which lead them to the necessity of a non-religious common sphere of ethics based on a "natural law" that is part of the lower storey (common kingdom) of reality. This superstructure then requires some kind of biblical justification.

Since the whole scheme of a common and redemptive kingdom is not obvious from a plain reading of Scripture, the distinction seems arbitrary. So how can this construct be theologically justified? The primary answer of the 2K proponents is grounded in a novel reading of the *Noahic covenant*. They claim that this covenant recapitulates creation (governed by general providence), and is, most critically, the *guarantor* of a *shared communal life of common values* among all men in the common kingdom. VanDrunen writes:

---

[20] Frame, *The Escondido Theology*, 142.

A two kingdoms doctrine distinguishes what is uniquely Christian from what is simply human.... Generally speaking to be human here and now means living in a common kingdom under the *Noahic covenant*. Christians share the life and activities of the common kingdom with all human beings. What differentiates them from the rest of humanity is their identification with the redemptive kingdom.[21]

As an inescapable consequence of this doctrine, culture (including civil society, family, education, state, art, the sciences, etc.), is a *common kingdom* phenomenon—composed of purely "human" norms, supposedly re-established in the Noahic covenant—and so we obviously cannot speak of *redeeming* it, because the language and restorative realities of the gospel do not transfer to the common order. It logically follows that we have no warrant to apply *special* revelation to the common kingdom with its common tasks and, consequently, no mandate to transform culture by the gospel. Thus VanDrunen writes, "We would do well, I believe, to discard familiar mantras about transformation and especially redemption. Nowhere does scripture call us to such grandiose tasks. They are human dreams rather than God-given obligations."[22]

Furthermore, since on this view the civic kingdom already shares the believers' norms in all "common" institutions and endeavours, it would be pointless to speak of redeeming something that isn't lost or sick and that requires no recovering or healing. Why redeem something that is already perfectly fitted to its task of being a purely temporary, non-religious sphere, occupied by believer and non-believer alike? It must be neutral or autonomous, on this basis, or else it *couldn't be common*. As a result of this theological construct, the incalculable task of dissecting all reality into *two kingdoms* becomes problematic for believers. Yet this massive project is to be undertaken on the highly insubstantial basis of a novel and implausible reading of God's covenant with Noah—a weight it certainly cannot bear.

The first time the word *covenant* is mentioned in Scripture is in Genesis 6:18. After the Flood, it is mentioned again (Genesis 9:11).

---

[21] VanDrunen, *Living in God's Two Kingdoms*, 167.
[22] VanDrunen, *Living in God's Two Kingdoms*, 171.

These instances are obviously connected. Yet, even earlier, in Genesis 6:8 we read, "But Noah found favor [*lit.* hen, *grace*] in the eyes of the Lord." We are specifically told that Noah was righteous and blameless and walked with God (Genesis 6:9). All these terms *presuppose* a covenant relationship already in existence between Noah and God. God's repeated reference to "my covenant" *is clearly a confirmation of an already existing one.* In the book of Genesis, the covenant is introduced to us as something with a fixed structure for a long period. The problem for the 2K proponents here is that if this covenantal language were referencing a covenant of "common grace" only (and "common grace" is a term the Bible never uses), then the first mention of any *covenant of grace* would be with Abraham in Genesis 12! This conclusion must surely be unacceptable to any Reformed believer, who sees atoning grace at work immediately after the Fall. Moreover, the text seems clear that this can't be the case because, as noted, God *renews* with righteous Noah a covenant that had already been in existence. It is God's ("My") covenant with Noah and his seed (Genesis 6:18).

It is abundantly clear that Genesis 6 reveals, not merely a *common* covenant of "nature," but a covenant that occupies an important place in the *redemptive history of salvation.* We should consider that the covenant renewal after the Flood included the following (see Genesis 8:15–9:17):

(a) The *sacrificial* offering of *clean* cattle and fowl (presupposes covenantal atonement with specified clean creatures).
(b) The Lord's acceptance of this world-sacrifice (Noah and his children were the only people alive at that point).
(c) The blessing on Noah and his sons repeating the original blessing pronounced in paradise.
(d) Clear stipulations concerning food (i.e. not eating meat with the blood still in it).
(e) The clear establishment of laws regarding manslaughter and murder and, therefore, the early origins of the state.
(f) A clear proclamation of sanctions for transgressing God's stipulations.
(g) Another repetition of blessing and covenant faithfulness for all creation.

(h) The promise that the Flood won't be repeated.
(i) And, finally, the rainbow as a sign of the covenant (notice what modern man has blasphemously done with that covenant sign today).

So, as we analyze the text, we notice covenantal blessing and judgement; we have offerings and sacrifices as the seal of covenant, which sets forth the terms of life and death basic to a blood covenant; finally, we have various stipulations spoken directly by special revelation to Noah as God's vassal. God is both the initiator and the guarantor of this covenant. Now, clearly, the *fruits* of this gracious covenant are also enjoyed, and have been enjoyed since the time of Noah and his sons, by the non-believer (Matthew 5:45; Acts 14:17), but that does not change the fact that it is a *covenant of grace*, with a critical place in the history of redemption. "Noah found grace in the eyes of the Lord" (Genesis 6:8). This cannot, therefore, be an aspect of so-called common grace, even though all creation is involved in this primeval act of God. Grace is never abstract, general and common, it is *always personal and covenantal*. As Cornelius van der Waal puts it:

It is not so that redemption *rests* on creation—nature does not form the first floor and grace the second. In God's gracious dealings with his people, all creation is involved. The "world sacrifice" Noah made foreshadowed the work of Jesus Christ. His unique and perfect sacrifice brings the restoration of all things, also the salvation of the eagerly longing creation.... We may not think of categories like "general" and "special" as if the covenant with Noah was a general covenant and that with Abraham a "special one." It is all or nothing. The whole of creation is for God's people and hence its use was given to Noah and his seed. But not to them as "general people" but as participants in the covenant. Those who disassociate themselves from the covenant, waive the right to re-creation.[23]

---

[23] Cornelius van der Waal, *The Covenantal Gospel* (Neerlandia, AB: Inheritance Publications, 1990), 28–29.

In an important sense, Noah leaves his country and its rebellious people and, like Abram, undertakes an exodus in the ark. As such, the ark is a type—a symbol—of salvation and a type of baptism, according to Peter—and baptism is the sign of the covenant of grace (1 Peter 3:18–21). Then, after leaving the ark as a new Adam and priest-king, Noah is recommissioned to obedience and the cultural mandate, in a manner precisely like Genesis 1:28.

The root of the 2K theological error seems, therefore, to lie in the idea that "creation" and "man" can be *generalized into abstractions*; God allegedly creates man "in general." But this is not the case, according to biblical revelation. The God of creation is the triune and redeeming God of Scripture, and he doesn't make "man in general"— this is precisely why Genesis 1–3 is an essential part of the gospel and contains its seed promise (Genesis 3:15). It is also why Scripture tells us that Christ is the second and last Adam, the truly obedient covenant Son. Creation and the Fall constitute the indispensable *historical prologue* of the gospel. Adam and Eve are not "man in general," occupying a common kingdom, they are God's vice-regents and vassals. Adam and Abel, Seth and Enoch, Noah and his sons, were all God's covenant men. Indeed, in the account of Noah the text uses the term "LORD God," which is his covenant name.

One is forced to ask the 2K proponents how many kingdoms there were before the covenant with Noah, if that covenant created or re-created a common kingdom? If there were already two kingdoms, which covenant established them? If there was only one kingdom before the Flood, was it redemptive or common? If for hundreds of years it was simply redemptive (despite all those non-believers in the world), why would we need a common kingdom now—what is the point of it? If it was simply one common kingdom before the flood, where then was grace? We see from this line of questioning that the 2K advocates run into all kinds of contorted and unscriptural reasoning in attempting to find these two kingdoms in Scripture.

The biblical reality is that God's covenant of grace is the foundation of history before and after the Flood. The LORD God was in relationship with man in his task and calling from the beginning. There was never a time when man as a race was left solely to "natural law" or general common principles to interpret his life and task. God spoke personally and immediately (special revelation) with particular people—Adam, Enoch and Noah—from the very beginning. Our first parents had the possibility of obeying God as his covenant partners—to be his image-bearers and dominion servants.

For Adam, the tree of the knowledge of good and evil was a symbol of God's power to judge obedience or disobedience. This is not to say that Adam, by obedience, could *earn salvation*. Adam needed to earn nothing in his original relationship with God. He was made upright, with nothing lacking, but he might *forfeit life* by disobedience. God's *creation covenant*, or, for want of a better term, *paradise covenant* with Adam was still between the Creator and Lord of all and a creature, and was thus a *covenant of grace*, whose terms were all established by God. To walk with God, as Adam and Eve initially did, is to live *by grace*. We should remember: the *good news* is that God is covenant Lord and king—that fact is basic to the *evangelion*. Even Adam and Eve had to believe that foundational truth by faith. Adam and Eve's obedience did not justify them. They simply lived by God's grace and favour. In other words, there has never been a "covenant of works" *as such*.

God calls all people from Adam and Noah in deep history, right up to the present time, to serve and obey him; he is the same God and remains unchanged. Further to that, the cultural mandate was a calling to develop and keep God's creation in obedience to him. That calling, basic to man as God's image-bearer, has not changed either. After his resurrection, Jesus Christ, the second Adam and true image-bearer, was mistaken for the gardener at the garden tomb, because he is also the true gardener, the true man of culture, who restores us to that original task of culture-making as prophets, priests and kings. The Christian calling is clearly not to live as monks in a cloister in a dualistic, bifurcated universe, where true spirituality is equated with institutional piety. We are God's ambassadors, calling creation to be reconciled to the King. We are not monastic pilgrims, cultural beggars, wandering the earth and pleading for a seat at the secular table. We are a royal priesthood in Christ, turning all the earth into God's sanctuary, for he owns the table!

In sum, the Noahic covenant is emphatically not a *general*, abstract covenant with creation or men "in general" that produces, via theological fiat, a *common kingdom*—there is no such "general man" and there is no such common kingdom.

THE SOCIOLOGICAL OR CULTURAL PROBLEM

The theological problem in 2K teaching is directly related to our final problem under consideration—the *sociological* or *cultural* problem. The Noahic covenant is invoked by 2K theologians, not simply as the basis for two alleged realms that don't mix, but, critically, as the basis for the *cultural homogeneity* (sameness) that we see around us—the common aspects of our activities and cultural life and the areas of agreement the Christian has with non-believers on moral and ethical issues. This argument is particularly important to analyze, because what gives 2K theology its apparent plausibility is not the cogency of its theological case regarding the Noahic covenant, but its rhetorical power, in the Western context, when highlighting morals and norms that seem largely common to all.

VanDrunen and other 2K advocates repeatedly argue that the elements of culture (state, education, society, family, business, trades, and much besides) all operate in a common way and in terms of common principles and values. With reference to politics, education and vocation, VanDrunen writes, "As an objective matter, the standards of morality and excellence in the common kingdom are ordinarily the same for believers and unbelievers: they share these standards in common under God's authority in the covenant with Noah."[24] In the same work, in reference to designing bridges, plumbing and so forth, VanDrunen argues that most things in life are just ordinary human activities carried out in the same manner by believer and unbeliever, "because God has upheld the natural order and sustained all human beings as his image-bearers through the Noahic covenant."[25]

As such, when Christians promote life, justice, truth, fair trade, honesty, faithfulness and the like, there is nothing distinctly Christian about these things, because they are grounded in the Noahic covenant—conceived as a generalized common covenant. On this basis, perhaps VanDrunen's most bizarre conclusion comes when he argues: "The odds are good, in fact, that if you ask your unbelieving neighbor whether he believes in freedom, satisfaction of basic needs, ecological responsibility, fair trade and healthy local businesses, he

---

[24] VanDrunen, *Living in God's Two Kingdoms*, 31.
[25] VanDrunen, *Living in God's Two Kingdoms*, 169.

will heartily agree."[26] This statement makes it obvious to me, at least, that these scholars advocating 2K theology need to leave their sheltered academic cloisters in Christianized, leafy communities in Escondido and Grand Rapids and go and live in the Islamic world for twelve months before promoting their doctrine. In fact, there is little need to go to Pakistan to question this assumption. Come to West Toronto and you can't get agreement from your neighbour on how many genders there are, or that marriage is between a man and a woman! Ask people in my progressivist neighbourhood about "freedom," in the sense of the Western political tradition, and they believe it is obsolete in light of the need for a socially just society. Talk to my neighbours about fair trade and they think that means an interventionist state with tariffs, quotas and market fixing. The 2K theorists at least believe the perceived "commonality" they experience with their neighbours is due to the *covenant with Noah*, and their entire argument is supposedly supported by this reading of Genesis. We have seen that their argument runs something like this: "We don't need to transform culture or creation with redemptive principles, because not only is this order headed for destruction (it will be replaced by re-creation so it's pointless, thus we should pray, grow spiritually and do evangelism), but the Noahic covenant guarantees that the 'common kingdom' shares our basic values anyway, so it has no need of healing or redeeming."

It is crucial to notice, first, that this is not what the covenant with Noah guarantees in the Genesis text. Rather, what non-believers benefit from in God's covenant of grace with Noah and his seed of faith is a promise of *stability* and *regularity*: seedtime and harvest, cold and heat, summer and winter, night and day. Moreover, God assures Noah that, despite the wickedness of men, he will never flood the earth again. This gracious covenant is *everlasting*, and God binds himself to this unalterable agreement for the blessing of all living creatures. Thus, the sun rises on the just and the unjust (Matthew 5:45). But where in the Genesis text is to be found a promise of shared cultural values and norms throughout time? Crucially, if this idea were explicit or implicit in this text, then we should expect, without fail, widespread homogeneity of cultural values and norms

---

[26] VanDrunen, *Living in God's Two Kingdoms*, 194.

amongst the human race—across all civilizations—since the time of Noah. Since God's promises cannot fail, VanDrunen and company must argue that there has been such homogeneity. Brian Mattson is rightly scathing in his criticism of this peculiar perspective:

> Few suggestions can be more historically ignorant and empirically false. To state the blindingly obvious: the history of the human race is not a history of cultural homogeneity. It is nothing but the record of cultures in conflict, most often resulting in warfare, bloodshed, persecution and slavery.[27]

It is plain to any serious observer of human life and culture that we have anything but a history of cultural sameness. The obvious choice, then, is either is to call God a liar or to acknowledge that the 2K view of Noah's covenant is wrong. History is the record of radical conflict of competing norms and values. Even today, in the West alone, we might consider that issues like abortion, human sexuality, marriage, criminal law, political doctrine and far-reaching philosophical ideas that shape every field of education (like evolution), show the complete lack of homogeneity in the things that matter most. The *evolutionary paradigm*, for example, has increasingly generated an intellectual climate and culture hostile to Christianity at almost every point in the West. And, just in the last century, where was the cultural homogeneity in Europe and beyond, with the rise of Hitler's Germany, Stalin's Russia, Mao's China, Pol Pot's Cambodia, Mussolini's Italy or the Ayatollah's Iran? Today, where is our commonality with the West's death cult, manifest in its wanton destruction of human life and the family?

We certainly have at least formal agreement with many nonbelievers about the reality and abiding character of physical laws, but this does not equate to *subjectively sharing the same norms, moral values and social expectations*. The simple fact is that Genesis 8 and 9 say *nothing* about whether my neighbour will understand and abide by God's Word-revelation in creation or Scripture, this passage simply assures me that God will stand by his covenant. Again, as Mattson has tellingly argued, VanDrunen tries to take a *prescriptive* text to

---

[27] Mattson, "Cultural Amnesia."

prove a morally *descriptive* point. But the covenant with Noah not only does not, it *cannot* explain whatever cultural agreement we have with non-believers.[28]

Despite this, the leading 2K teachers like VanDrunen, Horton and Tuininga want to tell us we don't need Christian transformation and redemption of culture, because there is no such mandate—and this is because, due to the Noahaic covenant, there is common agreement among men about norms and cultural questions, both in the past and in our present culture. Yet what is, in fact, notable about the considerable agreement we certainly have enjoyed in recent centuries in the West is that it is clearly the *exception in history*, rather than the rule! Ironically, the actual historical reason for cultural homogeneity, to the degree that we observe it today in the English-speaking world and among the European nations that were part of what we once called Christendom, is found in the very place VanDrunen and company least want to look—in the Christian evangelization of the West and the gospel's impact on culture. To put it bluntly, the reason you and I eat stir-fried chicken, rather than drinking the blood of the dead and consuming stir-fried man-flesh, is *because of Christianity*. Charles Darwin actually made this very point about the impact of Christianity in his journal during voyages in the Pacific Islands.[29]

The undeniable reality is that, for most of history, the majority of societies have lived in ways antithetical to God's law and the Christian gospel, not in terms of common norms and values derived from a scholastically-conceived natural law (see Romans 1). Fallen men have supressed the truth in unrighteousness and applied their depraved minds to all the socio-cultural arts, creating cultures and civilizations hostile to God and revealed truth. This is not unexpected or surprising to us, since Paul tells us that man in his fallen state cannot and will not submit himself to God's law (Romans 8:7). As a result, if you go to Pakistan today, where I have travelled many times and where my family lived for seventeen years, the odds are not good that your neighbour will share your Christian view that the genitals of a little girl should not be mutilated, or that a man should not have up to four wives and beat them at his leisure.

---

[28] Mattson, "Cultural Amnesia."

[29] See Joseph Boot, *The Mission of God: A Manifesto of Hope for Society Today* (Toronto: Ezra Press & Wilberforce Publications, 2016), 381–382.

Historically, the odds were not good for the pioneering missionary to India, William Carey, that his neighbour would agree with him that his wife should not be burned alive on his funeral pyre, and so he worked tirelessly to get the barbarous practice of *sati* banned. And even in the West itself, in Britain, the mother of all parliamentary democracy, man-theft and enslavement were socially approved until men like William Wilberforce, in the name of gospel and covenant, worked for a lifetime to have it outlawed.

In sum, as Mattson has memorably pointed out, attacking explicitly Christian engagement to *transform culture* as unnecessary because we already have shared cultural values is like attacking the use of the *polio vaccine* as unnecessary because no one has polio. The only reason men don't have polio is because of the vaccine. And the only reason there is any cultural agreement in the West today is because our evangelical forebears ignored as worthless the kind of arguments made by earlier formulations of 2K pietism. What makes such anti-vaccination movements possible? "Forgetfulness. Amnesia. The blessing of a vaccine can be its curse. It enables its beneficiaries to take their health so for granted that we find them arguing against the very thing that preserves their health."[30]

2K'S THREE SHORTCOMINGS

I have argued that the 2K teaching suffers from three serious problems: a philosophical, a theological and a cultural problem. *Firstly*, a philosophically dualistic and unbiblical bifurcation of reality divides up God's creation into a *common order* (to be historically destroyed) and a *spiritual, ecclesiastical realm* (to be redeemed)—with the human body alone barely managing to escape out of this common order at the end of history. Creation and re-creation form two essentially unrelated realms and ages. As a result, there is a total failure in 2K thought to understand the *radicality* and unity of God's creative, redemptive purposes in history! For, in Scripture, there is no generalized creation, no general abstract man, nor a general common order; there is no natural law or reason that operates independent of, or unrelated to, special revelation; nor is there a non-religious space that is not created, governed and controlled by an undivided

---

[30] Mattson, "Cultural Amnesia."

God in an undivided created order. At all times, God covenantally relates and speaks to his creatures as his image-bearers and intended lords of creation.

Secondly, I have argued that the primary (though not only) theological problem with this doctrine is seen in a misinterpretation of the *Noahic covenant*. In 2K theology, that special covenant of grace with Noah is misused to manufacture two kingdoms (the common and redemptive) by theological fiat. This theological fiction is then utilized to give plausibility to a supposed *subjective agreement* that believers and non-believers are thought to have in all the "common kingdom" spheres of *politics, law, family, education, ethics* and so forth. Here, there is a serious failure to appreciate the radicality of the Fall. Man is, in fact, a sinner who is hostile to God's law and will not obey from the heart without regeneration.

Thirdly, we have seen that the historic areas of cultural agreement present in Western history are not the result of Noah's covenant, but largely the product of the Christian evangelization of society—areas of agreement that are now rapidly eroding. As the underlying religious consensus evaporates, so does our historic social cohesion. The failure of 2K thinkers to appreciate the *radicality of the Fall* results in them drawing the line through reality in the wrong place. The biblical line delineating two kingdoms is found in the condition of the *heart of man* (a direction of heart, not a dualistic arrangement of reality) and is expressed and worked out in all his familial, social and cultural pursuits. The condition of the heart of man determines membership in either the kingdom of light or the kingdom of darkness. Certainly, the church has a special place in God's kingdom reign as *his bride* (the chosen image for the church in Scripture), but the church is not the only institution identified with that kingdom, nor can the kingdom of God be reduced to it.

This failure of comprehension regarding the radicality of both creation and the Fall of man has lead us to the third problem—the cultural or sociological problem—where the radicality of redemption is also denied. We have seen that, for 2K thought, most of the important matters of life, including education, family, art, music, politics, social order, law and much besides, are handed over to a *common realm*, free from the workings of redemptive-transformative grace and special revelation. This common order is still said by the 2K proponents to be governed by God (whatever that actually means in such a context), so that it now appears that God is divided, having different sets of norms and moral values depending on which area of life you are operating in.

In reality, the so-called *common kingdom* is effectively handed over to Satan and his ideologies (like evolutionism, Islamism, paganism, occultism, scientism, pluralism, multiculturalism, existentialism and every other "ism") for him to rule in the place of Christ and his inscripturated Word. And, since the family and the school are also falsely located within the "common kingdom," somehow Paul's teachings to Christians concerning marriage as the key to understanding our covenantal union with Christ are relegated to the non-redemptive kingdom. My marriage, *as marriage*, and family, *as family*, are outside of the redemptive kingdom! In short, 2K theology fails to appreciate the radicality of redemption—*the cosmic reconciliation of all things to God*. This is precisely why VanDrunen is anxious to deny the scriptural worldview of Creation-Fall-Redemption in terms of one kingdom of God. But this unbiblical limitation of redemption leaves the Christian in a schizophrenic position. Since history and Scripture prove that the so-called *common kingdom* makes a strong effort to crush those seeking to advance God's redemptive kingdom, is God at war with himself? Is the believer not at war with himself in the different spheres? If not, and it is merely Satan using the common kingdom to attack the redemptive kingdom, how does God go about changing that common kingdom, so that it ceases to assault, attack and oppress the redemptive kingdom, and thereby rescue his people from their oppression, since grace and special revelation are not allowed to transform it? The 2K teaching on creation and redemption is caught in a hopeless and irresolvable conflict.

REAL-WORLD IMPLICATIONS

The implications of all this are far-reaching. Where does 2K theology really leave Christian political organizations, advocacy groups, legal centres, pregnancy crisis centres and adoption agencies, charities, Christian schools and universities, guilds and professional organizations? The 2K answer is that they cannot be distinctly Christian and redemptive, because they are part of a common kingdom that is destined to be destroyed. Furthermore, they are essentially pointless, since there is no such thing as a distinctly Christian education, law, political position, charity or other endeavour in the common kingdom. All such efforts by Christians are *non-transformational* and *non-redemptive activities* of secondary importance and can all be done in happy cooperation with non-believers and their values. Yet nothing could be more obvious than the fact that the heart and, thereby, worldview of the believer entail a radically different approach to family, education, politics, art, law and life, in terms of the lordship of Jesus Christ and the totality of his Word—and history proves this to be the case. A Christian and non-Christian artist may both use the same pots of paint and canvas, but what they say with their art will be radically different. Compare Bach and Mendelssohn with Holst or John Cage, or contrast Rembrandt with Picasso and see what you find. The structure of the oil paint or the number of notes they had to work with was the same, but the direction of the art is radically different.

Michael Horton, an important popularizer of the 2K doctrine, in his rather obtuse and angry book, *Beyond Culture Wars: Is America a Mission Field or Battlefield?* (the title exhibiting yet another 2K false dichotomy), is flippant about matters of incredible import within a world he predictably claims is simply to be destroyed.[31] Dismissing the pejoratively-labelled "culture wars" as more concerned with abortion than personal evangelism, he suggests that a professing Christian's opinion on the life issue is a matter of very little consequence, asking: "Doesn't anyone care about the only important question here: What does he believe about Christ?"[32] This illustrates with frightening clarity the dire problem with the 2K bifurcation of reality. Horton manifests his enculturation in secular thought when he views abortion as a legal and political matter that is, therefore, part of the "common kingdom." That is to say, state-sanctioned murder is a matter for the *common kingdom* to deal with (where we apparently enjoy cultural homogeneity!); it is not for the *redemptive kingdom* to interfere in such matters, and so we shouldn't work *as a church* with petitions or social engagement to seek the end of the

---

[31] Michael Horton, *Beyond Culture Wars: Is America a Mission Field or Battlefield?* (Chicago: Moody, 1994), 21.

[32] Horton, *Beyond Culture Wars*, 33.

murder of the unborn as a priority. For Horton, what a professing Christian man believes about abortion is relatively unimportant. What really matters is what that person believes about Christ (the spiritual and redemptive kingdom). So we see that this two-storey worldview creates false dichotomies everywhere—as though what a man believes about abortion doesn't say something important about who he believes Christ really is and what he believes about the status of God's revealed Word.

The grand irony in all this is that it is in fact 2K proponents who have *politicized the church* and ecclesiasticized the Word of God. By excluding politics from direct service to the Word of God, it reveals that it has politicized the church with politicized members. Christians have their own political ideas and opinions, and 2K thinking refuses to bring all that under the light of God's Word to be judged by Christ. Politicized Christians become very angry when their profaned politics come under the light of God's truth. In light of this threat, the 2K-influenced churchmen want to avoid service to God's Word at that point, lest their people be upset or even leave. This is a prime example of politics determining life in the church! Because here, politics is permitted to lord it over the pulpit, bullying it into silence, truncating God and his Word and denying his authority in the life of the church—thus the world exercises dominion over Christ's church. The 2K advocates piously demand the "purity of preaching," by which they mean a preaching free from political taints and implications—they want nothing to do with politics. Zuidema's insight here is dazzling:

> Supposedly the pulpit is too sacred, but in reality the member is too secular politically and the servant of the Word, in the measure that he gives in to this carnal dictatorship, is too unfaithful in his service of Jesus Christ. The worship service in which politics is excluded is the worship service where politics exercises dominion over God's word...and where the gospel is crippled.... If the church will have nothing to do with politics, then one can be certain that a radically worldly politics has already forced itself imperiously to within the very walls of the church.... Ecclesiastical and political questions and actions cannot be severed from man's heart religion and his love service

to God.... The word of God [if severed] then becomes ecclesiasticized and the church then places itself central instead of
the Word of God. Certainly the worst that can happen, if the
church is placed central, is that service to God's Word, entrusted to the church, is perverted to a service of God's Word to the
church, and its ecclesiastical exercise of power is politicized to
its very core.... It [then] demands an axiological splitting of
reality into a higher, specifically ecclesiastical area of authority,
and a lower and therefore religiously inferior area of authority
of "temporal" politics, as a result it automatically becomes
"secular" and is regarded as being at least more "secular" and
less "religious" than that special ecclesiastical character of the
spiritual authority.... Inescapably, such a church equates itself
with the Word of God, which is entrusted to it for service. At
the same time however, life outside of the church, including that
of the state and political parties, is in this manner abandoned to
the law of the so-called pragmatic.... The ecclesiasticizing of
religion necessarily calls into being the profaning of the
non-ecclesiastical area.[33]

This remarkable insight was penned over forty years ago, and yet it
accurately plots the trajectory of the 2K theological scheme: politics
being pushed out of the church; a dualistic scheme established; the
profaning and secularization of the political sphere; the church
becoming central, making the Word a service to the church alone,
and the consequent reality of a politicized congregation that will not
tolerate its political and social ideas being brought under the light of
God's Word. It would be difficult to find a more apt description of
the modern evangelical church.

The scriptural response to 2K pietism must be that of Colossians 1
and Ephesians 1. God's work of *redemption* in these programmatic
texts is much wider than personal salvation and a place in heaven
while "spiritual people" wait for *parousia*. Instead, since all creation
is implicated in the Fall, so *all creation must be redeemed* (Romans
8:18–25). Christ died to redeem everything that sin polluted. "The

---

33 S.U. Zuidema, *Communication and Confrontation* (Assen/Kampen, Netherlands:
Royal VanGorcum, 1972), 38–42.

sweep of redemption is as comprehensive as the sweep of sin," as Cornelius Van Til once put it.[34] As such, all creation must be sanctified by the death and resurrection of Jesus—there can be no sacred-secular divide, no common and redemptive dichotomy. This means that addressing the social and cultural destruction of a people via such evils as same-sex "marriage," sexual slavery, pornography, abortion, euthanasia, prostitution, child abuse, state-sanctioned theft and much more, is part of the Christian, redemptive calling as a royal priesthood. Redemption certainly does not encompass all *individuals*, but it is *cosmic* (Romans 4:13)!

Our true destiny is not a "spiritual" home in heaven. The apostle John tells us in Revelation 21:1–4 that at the consummation, the *New Jerusalem* comes down to a redeemed earth, and God descends to dwell with men. *We were made for earth and so God is restoring and expanding Eden.* As a result, we are not escape artists, but stewards. As Andrew Sandlin has powerfully put it, "For Christians to surrender redemption anywhere is eventually to surrender it everywhere."[35] God's creation is not a merely probationary order, with no enduring significance. It is God's world, along with everything in it, and it is the only creation there is (Psalm 24:1). Though it is surely fallen, God has not abandoned it, but restores and redeems it through Jesus Christ. And we are his ambassadors with the message of reconciliation (2 Corinthians 5:20). We go out into the world in Christ's absolute authority, to disciple and teach the nations God's total Word for all of life. It follows that to abandon this task is treason to the King.

Moreover, the purpose of the church and our worship is not, finally, to keep grace *in the church*, but for it to flow out from us, for the healing of the nations (Ezekiel 47:12). The Christ of Psalm 2 commands all kings and rulers to submit to him as Lord and Messiah (not as an abstract governor employing natural law), and Daniel sees the uncut altar-stone that is Christ and his kingdom smashing all the empires of men and becoming a *mountain filling the earth*. The prophet Habakkuk declares: "The earth shall be filled with the

---

[34] Cornelius Van Til, *Christian Theistic Ethics* (Phillipsburg: P & R Publishing, 1980), 86–87.

[35] P. Andrew Sandlin, "Christian Redemption: Individual or Cosmic?" (unpublished research essay, 2016).

knowledge of the glory of the Lord as the waters cover the sea" (2:14). Thus, we cannot contain or restrict God's redemptive work to the institution of the church—it breaks out to transform all things. And this work begins in us now. "For if any man is in Christ he is a new creation" (2 Corinthians 5:17). The kingdom of God has already arrived in Jesus Christ, and this gospel of the kingdom is forcefully advancing, growing like a mustard seed into a great tree, and working like leaven affecting the whole loaf, until it fills all creation. We must then conclude that every Christian (including the scholar) is obligated to take every thought captive and bring all things, in every part of life, into subjection to Jesus Christ. As Herman Dooyeweerd has put it:

> If there is a *dialectical tension* between the nature of divine creation and the Christian faith, one should at least demonstrate it with unambiguous citations from God's word. Otherwise we run the risk of mixing philosophical speculation into the very heart of Christian doctrine.... Christian scholars today face a choice. Either they acknowledge that nothing in this temporal world can be withdrawn from the claim of the Christian religion and that this religion will not be content with the role of a decorative superstructure atop a scholarship that is at bottom and in essence idolatrous. Or they should withdraw from a field where they are deeply convinced the banner of Christ's kingship cannot be boldly planted. No other choice exists.[36]

Since nothing in all creation can be withdrawn from the claims of Christ, and his Word-revelation cannot be reduced to a decorative border to idolatrous thinking, we are called to a radically Christian life. Anything less is a failure to sell everything to buy the pearl of great price.

The "churchification" (ecclesiasticization) of Christianity in our time, to which the 2K theology is now a significant contributor, has called into being a profaned public space. Zuidema draws out the grave danger in this posture:

---

36 Herman Dooyeweerd, cited in Marcel E. Verburg, *Herman Dooyeweerd: The Life and Work of a Christian Philosopher* (Grand Rapids: Paideia Press, 2015), 159.

The ecclesiasticized church calls into being a secularized 'world' which cannot rest until it in its turn has subjected to itself this ecclesiasticized church; until it has subjected the ecclesiasticized Bible use to a secularized Bible use which rejects the ecclesiasticized authority of the Bible and therefore, in its opinion, fundamentally rejects all authority of the Bible.[37]

Today, the church in the West is already far down this road. Our only hope is a recovery of a full-orbed gospel and integral Christian view of all of life, where we as God's people, entrusted with the precious gift of the Word of God, again bring the witness of that Word to *every* corner of creation.

---

[37] Zuidema, *Communication and Confrontation*, 42.

5

THE SCRIPTURAL MOTIVE: THE KINGDOM OF GOD

THEN TO HIM WAS GIVEN DOMINION AND GLORY AND A
KINGDOM, THAT ALL PEOPLES, NATIONS, AND LANGUAGES
SHOULD SERVE HIM. HIS DOMINION IS AN EVERLASTING
DOMINION, WHICH SHALL NOT PASS AWAY, AND HIS
KINGDOM THE ONE WHICH SHALL NOT BE DESTROYED
(DANIEL 7:14).

So far in this study of the nature of the cultural challenge facing the
Christian church, we have seen a spiritual force active throughout
the political and cultural life of the West that is seeking the eradication
of man as God's image-bearer and the radical reduction of orthodox
Christian faith to an irrelevant and outmoded form of spirituality,
with no place in the public square. We have also considered the validity
of the dualistic response to this challenge popular in evangelicalism

today—a "two kingdoms" theology offered to the church to cope with the evident dissonance between scriptural faith and the various strands of humanism all around us, which have emphatically de-Christianized, and now dominate, the public space.

The Reformed scholar Evan Runner rightly identified the dangerous outcome of accepting *any variety* of a "two kingdoms" bifurcation of reality:

> Fundamentally, the nature-grace position is one of *accommodation*: the insights of the non-Christian can be accommodated and taken over by the Christian as long as they are based on reason and not on biased ideologies.... Wherever the nature-grace vision is accepted, one encounters different accommodations with non-Christian thought and practice, because there is no specifically Christian criterion with which one might judge what suits the realm of nature best.[1]

We have seen that this loss of a criterion is a fatal flaw. If there is no distinctly Christian basis for the believer's thought and action in ordinary life in the world, then the Christian is confronted with two dilemmas. First, we are handed over to endless divisions among Christians, casting about in a sea of cultural relativism, frantically drafting peace treaties with non-Christian thought (and reaching diverse solutions); such a scenario leads to a massive expansion of the "secular" realm, by radically restricting the applicability of biblical truth to an ever-shrinking "sacred" realm. On this view, anyone who wants to be *distinctly Christian* must pursue a "sacred vocation" or "sacred scholarship," for everything else is rendered profane, neutral or common. Here, Christian service only takes place within the domain of the institutional "church." The outcome of this thought process on the scope and applicability of the gospel is utterly stifling and its implications for culture are devastating.

The problem is, whether it is the "two kingdoms" of one of the various permutations of scholasticism, or the "two kingdoms" of the Anabaptist tradition with its victimization mentality and pacifistic

---

[1] Evan Runner, *Walking in the Way of the Word: The Collected Writings of Evan Runner*, vol. 2 (Grand Rapids: Paideia Press, 2009), xxiii-xxiv.

sojourn through an alien world, "two kingdoms" teaching in the modern church is ubiquitous. The first form emphasizes two separate realms (whether ontological or eschatological), the latter, two separate cultures:

> [T]he Anabaptists are unanimous in maintaining that the kingdom of this world and the kingdom of Christ unfold in terms of two separate cultures and two distinct histories—the history of a fallen world and the history of a redeemed world. There is no intrinsic connection between these two cultures and histories until the final Day of Judgment.[2]

The modern Western church has blended these historic *two kingdoms views* into a new, retreatist pottage to feed a weak, ineffectual, intellectually impotent, compromised and complacent church culture of inward Christian pansies—a Christian culture, I would venture to say, that would be unrecognizable as truly Christian by our militant Puritan forebears.

In the face of the undeniable decay of the Christian faith and church in our time in the West, we desperately need a recovery of a truly scriptural view of life:

> Redemption is not the reparation of a defect occasioned by the fall and resulting in the loss of the image of God, as the nature-grace position holds. Nor is redemption the start of a new project by God because his first one of creation really failed, as the Anabaptist position holds.[3]

What is in fact needed is a recovery of a scriptural confessional vision that "rejects both the dualism inherent in the nature-grace position, which confines redemption to the realm of grace, and the two kingdom position of the Anabaptist, which limits God's reconciliation to the community of the faithful."[4] The truly biblical vision we so need to recover is nothing less than a *full-orbed gospel*: a vision that takes God at his Word (in its totality) and understands and applies the implications

---

[2] Runner, *Walking in the Way*, xxvi-xxvii.
[3] Runner, *Walking in the Way*, xxix.
[4] Runner, *Walking in the Way*, xxix.

of the resurrection of Jesus Christ to all of life. A gospel of redemption that restores creation as the *theatre of God's glory.*

GOOD NEWS?

It is necessary, then, to return to the rudiments. The gospel (Grk. Ευαγγέλιο/*Euaggelion*) quite literally means "good news." But news that is good is not delivered into a vacuum, nor is it comprehensible without a *context.* News can only be *good* in relation to a broader story. For example, imagine you are given the news: "the battle is ended," or "the patient is out of danger," or "the fire is out," or "the baby has been born," or "the house has been sold." All these headlines *presuppose* a wider story within which the news might be understood to be truly *good.* After all, "the house has been sold" or "the fire is out" could be bad news, if they referred to the home you had been hoping to buy or the open fire in the hearth of your family room on a freezing cold night. In other words, more expansive back-stories are needed to provide a wider context for these headlines, in which the news might be seen to be *good* news.

Although the phrase has become trite and trendy in some circles, and is often misapplied, as Christians we are rightly "centred on the gospel" (or "gospel-centred") and, consequently, taken up with both understanding and sharing the good news. We increasingly do this, however, in a church and world that have *lost the context* of the wider story. As a result, it is increasingly difficult for the non-believer to make sense of Christian *gospel headlines*, to really recognize the gospel as good news. Most biblically orthodox believers understand the kernel of the gospel to be the good news that the salvation of sinners is accomplished by Jesus Christ, through his death for our sin and resurrection from the grave. This means that, by repentance and faith, we are rescued from the judgment we each deserve for our sins, and so the way is opened to heaven. This account is correct as far as it goes, but as the evangelical cultural theologian Andrew Sandlin has pointed out, it doesn't go far enough: "This common description is necessary, but not sufficient. You can't have the gospel without it, but you need more than this to have the gospel."[5]

---

5   P. Andrew Sandlin, "Reclaiming Culture is Gospel Ministry," in *Jubilee* 15 (Fall 2015): 4.

In a sense, this truncated formulation of the gospel, which may make sense to a biblically-literate Christian, is a *headline version* of the gospel, without a context—a wider story within which to understand one's personal salvation from the guilt and corruption of sin. Again, as Sandlin has correctly observed, "The Gospel doesn't start with the cross, or resurrection, though these are its high points. The gospel starts with the Creation and Fall."[6] It is therefore only when we start to plot the course of the gospel as the *road from Eden* that we begin to comprehend its full scope and meaning and, therefore, its full *significance* in our lives—its truly awe-inspiring goodness.

In Scripture, Christ is set forth as the *Alpha* and the *Omega*, the beginning and the end, the fullness of God's purposes and the very creator and restorer of all things, such that we must not relegate his salvific and redemptive role in world history to a brief earthly appearance and then a great intervention at the end. These are major movements in God's masterpiece, but not the whole symphony. Christ is both the beginning and end, but he also dominates everything in between.

Some might object that in this process of expounding the fullness of the gospel, we are making what is simple complicated and demanding, instead of the "old-time," simple gospel of personal salvation. But this is both a lazy anti-intellectualism and an aspect of the unhealthy democratic impulse to reduce everything to the lowest common denominator. The reality is, there is no such thing as a simplistic gospel that disregards the grand story or worldview of Scripture. Such a characterization of the gospel constitutes a fallacy of simplicity and results in a *distortion* of the gospel, rather than its clarification. The oft-heard phrase in evangelicalism, "Jesus died for you and has a plan for your life," is not the gospel. It is only when we cease to view the gospel in a purely individualistic and reductionist fashion and see it instead in light of *all* Scripture, that the full beauty, glory and goodness of the gospel is seen.

THE EXISTENTIAL CONTEXT

It is important to insist that the gospel is neither an abstract concept —merely a high-sounding *idea*, like the monistic world of Plotinus'

---

6 Sandlin, "Reclaiming Culture," 4.

absolute One—nor is it simply a personal spiritual experience or reality. The gospel is not adequately expounded by my personal testimony, as though it were essentially an autobiographical element within the wider story of *my* life. Instead, in the fullest sense, the gospel of God's kingdom is the very backdrop, stage and theatre within which all of life, for every individual, is lived. This is true, then, of both the believer and the non-believer, whether they realize it or not. For one person, the gospel is the savour of life and, to another, the savour of death (2 Corinthians 2:16). Yet, before we encounter the person of Jesus and the cross of Christ in his *specific work* of historical satisfaction for sin, we find the human race alive in God's creation, in the context of a meta-story of kingship, justice and redemption.

The creation itself, as the necessary foundation of the story, is good. In fact, everything that was made was pronounced to be *very good* by God himself (Genesis 1:31). This is actually the first *good news* we discover in Scripture. Creation, as God's creation, is inherently good, not evil. This means that the material creation in itself (of which human persons are a part) is not the reason we need and preach salvation in Jesus. The created order is not the *cause* of our disquiet, neither is it a problem to be overcome. The essential human need, according to the Bible, is *not* to escape from or transcend creation, as though it were a drag on human existence. We have already seen in this study that various Indo-European worldviews have suggested that the body is a prison, or that the material world is a lower and debased form of existence, and that, in order to grasp salvation, one must be liberated from the body and material world into a realm of pure spirit, being, ideas or abstract forms.

However, if creation is indeed good, as Scripture affirms, why the disquiet in the human heart and anxiety in human experience? Why the universal longing for salvation or redemption and a quest for true "spirituality"? Why the desire for liberation and the necessity of escape from the burden of life? One poet has captured the lurking sense of dread:

> Thus far, thus dead. The clock
> Strikes death, ticks time
> To die, to die, to stock

The Grave, to prime
The pump of vengeance
To full flow. The knocking
Rain, against all vigilance
Seeps in. The clocking
  Death rides high…[7]

Man is a broken being, conscious of the ravages of time and history. The *gospel* is a story within time, sovereignly ordained from eternity, which begins with the *good news* of a good creation, but in which that good and Edenic order is disrupted and disturbed and falls into ruin. This *Fall* was not from spirit into matter—it wasn't metaphysical at all—it was a fall from righteousness, holiness and godly dominion in covenantal intimacy with God, into the sin of idolatry (creation worship), with a resulting distortion, decay and disruption of every aspect of life, because of the severing of relationship with God. In other words, the fall of our race was *ethical*, and so the human problem lies in the heart of man, manifesting itself in *all* his actions and activities.

Fundamentally alienated from intimacy with God and disjoined from his *proper calling*, man is lost, cut off from paradise in the apparent wilderness of time, so that, concurrent and intermixed with the joys of life, come disquieting realities that traumatize him and make him yearn for release. In this sense, man has a homing beacon that signals his origins in Eden, even when he is not conscious of the truth of the biblical account. The writer of Ecclesiastes captures the post-Edenic existential reality best:

For everything there is a season, and a time for every matter
      under heaven:
  a time to be born, and a time to die;
  a time to plant, and a time to pluck up what is planted;
  a time to kill, and a time to heal;
  a time to break down, and a time to build up;
  a time to weep, and a time to laugh;

---

7 Rousas John Rushdoony, "The Clock Strikes Death," in *The Luxury of Words: Poems of Rousas John Rushdoony* (Vallecito, CA: Chalcedon, Ross House Books, 2003), 84.

a time to mourn, and a time to dance;
a time to cast away stones, and a time to gather stones
    together;
a time to embrace, and a time to refrain from embracing;
a time to seek, and a time to lose;
a time to keep, and a time to cast away;
a time to tear, and a time to sew;
a time to keep silence, and a time to speak;
a time to love, and a time to hate;
a time for war, and a time for peace.
What gain has the worker from his toil? I have seen the business that God has given to the children of man to be busy with. He has made everything beautiful in its time. Also, he has put eternity into man's heart, yet so that he cannot find out what God has done from the beginning to the end (Ecclesiastes 3:1–11).

There are good beginnings, and yet, because of sin, also painful endings with all things. Moreover, we see the decay and distortion of everything touched by the reality of man's rebellion. Zack Eswine, in his imaginative and insightful book on the message of Ecclesiastes, tell us:

> In the Garden of Eden, God told Adam and Eve ahead of time what they could expect regarding the landscape of their days. He told them about the land, the animals, their love for each other, their food, work, and the absence of any need to lock their doors at night. He also told them of two trees, two kinds of life, and the possibility of death should one of these trees experience misuse by them. Then after the death came, God prepared them ahead of time regarding how their days east of Eden would change (Genesis 3:16–19).[8]

This historic reality is what leads to the present *mixed experience* of humanity, described so evocatively in Ecclesiastes 3. Trauma, tragedy and disquiet now share space with times of delight, repose

---

[8]   Zack Eswine, *Recovering Eden: The Gospel According to Ecclesiastes* (Phillipsburg: P & R Publishing, 2014), 122.

and contentment. Death, killing, weeping, mourning, tearing down, losing, hatred and war are mingled with laugher and birth, dancing and building. Thus, we cannot speak truthfully about our lives, our desires and fears, our human experience, without reference to the *inescapable* reality of time and history and confronting its traumatic dimension—despite the fact that many philosophies would have us deny reality and teach that life is but a passing illusion. We simply cannot elude the world nor evacuate creation, for "there is a time for every matter and every work" (Ecclesiastes 3:17), including the work of facing the human condition.

Scripture is plain, then, that in the beginning, in Eden, there was nothing about time (history) that was our enemy or caused us distress:

> Time was like a friend who allows us to spend a weekend of retreat in his home. Within this provision, we could recover and live out our purpose. Time was a living room for company, a hallway for movement, a bedroom for lovemaking and rest, a table for food, a yard for work and play, a path for reflection. Time was beautiful; a friend to humanity as both it and they co-habited the God-given world.[9]

The tragedy of life now, in this fallen world, is that time seems to stalk and haunt us with innumerable pressures and stresses. It exposes our boredom, rots the rafters of our security and tarnishes the finish on our most prized experiences. And—like a once-beautiful and majestic stately home with welcoming grounds that in former times could have taken your breath away but now lies dilapidated and in ruins, surrounded by signs saying "No trespassing"—Eden is out of reach. Yet the desire to return still runs in our veins—we remember our home still, though its image fades like a picture postcard. This is because eternity is still in our hearts. Yet now, because of sin, the precious gift of time becomes the theatre of our judgement. Creation is placed under a curse, bearing the marks of sin's pollution (Genesis 3:17–19), and human life is marked by frustration, fear and restlessness.

---

9 Eswine, *Recovering Eden*, 125.

THE OFFICE-BEARER

The reason we have something to speak into culture as Christians, however, something far more significant than any poetic reflection on human alienation, is because there is much more to the gospel. It begins *historically* with creation and the Fall, but it rests on an agreement from eternity past. This agreement of the divine council is first spoken of in Eden when, as the curse is pronounced, a promise is also made; the seed of the woman is going to crush the serpent's head, and the serpent shall bruise his heel (Genesis 3:15). Theologians often call this the great *protoevangel*. The curse is to be broken and the process of death will start working backwards, as C.S. Lewis once put it.[10] Thus, in the Old Testament, through his tears and sorrow, amid the disquiet and tragedy of his ravaged days, the ancient suffering patriarch Job looked to that promise in hope: "For I know that my redeemer lives, and at the last he will stand upon the earth. And after my skin has been thus destroyed, yet in my flesh I shall see God, whom I shall see for myself, and my eyes shall behold and not another" (Job 19:25–27). Who is this Redeemer from the destruction of sin and death, and the derelictions of ill-spent and wasted time? Jesus Christ. As Scripture says, "Time has waited long enough. God sends forth his son" (Galatians 4:4).

At this point we must pause before rushing with exuberant haste to the great events of Jesus' life recorded in the Gospels, because Jesus comes with a *context*—an historical one. It is this context that helps us truly to grasp the scope and implications of the *good news*. The gospel is first disclosed repeatedly in the Old Testament, and it is in terms of this biblical prophetic witness that Jesus understood both himself and his mission. The apostle Paul quotes from Isaiah 52 in Romans 10:15: "How beautiful upon the mountains are the feet of Him who brings good news [gospel]." The prophet is reminding the oppressed covenant people that one day the full outworking of deliverance and salvation by the might of their King will take place: "The Lord has bared His holy arm before the eyes of all the nations, and all the ends of the earth shall see the salvation of our God" (Isaiah 52: 10). Here Scripture makes plain that *God is King* of all the nations

---

[10] C.S. Lewis, *The Lion, The Witch and The Wardrobe*, vol. 2: The Chronicles of Narnia (reprint; New York: HarperCollins, 2008).

and the entire earth will witness his great salvation in history. Scripture is equally clear that this salvation is accomplished only by the person of Jesus Christ the Lord. It is precisely this fact that makes it critically important not to trifle with the name of the Lord Jesus Christ, nor rush without thought to the life of Jesus.

The title *Christ* is a translation of the Hebrew word *Messiah*, meaning *the anointed one*, who is ordained and sent by God for a particular purpose. We must remember that when the Old Testament first speaks of *Messiah*, the name of *Jesus* is not yet known. He was announced as Messiah *before* he came historically as Jesus Christ. This is important, because the *good news* does not begin with the birth of Jesus, as is so often assumed. Moreover, even in the gospels, we are not strictly given a "life of Jesus" (for many of the details of his life are of little concern to the gospel writers), for the simple reason that he cannot be separated from Old Testament prophecy, from the Old Testament expectation of Messiah, and thus from the salvation-history out of which he came, according to God's eternal plan. As the Dutch theologian Klaas Schilder puts it:

No one is able to characterise the name of Jesus in a faithful way, as long as it has not become clear to him from the whole of Scripture what Jesus came to accomplish as the Christ and what he therefore, as God's office-bearer *par excellence*, has to do in, and for, and also with the cosmos.[11]

The gospel is not simply what Christ has come to do *for us* individually (i.e. forgive my personal sins and grant me a place in the kingdom of heaven), but also what he has come to do *with us* and *with his world*, as our Creator, King and covenant head. Paul says of God the Son, the Messiah, "For from him and through him and to him are all things" (Romans 11:36). He thus dominates, directs and governs all ages within the scheme of the gospel, because God is working out a plan and purpose for all history, which is summed up in Christ.

In short, Jesus presents himself to us *in his own light* in Scripture, and it is in his work as the Christ that he manifests that he is God's *prophet, priest and king* who has come to reconcile back to God all

---

[11] Klaas Schilder, *Christ and Culture* (Winnipeg: Premier, 1977), 12.

things that were alienated. We cannot construct a "Jesus" and "salvation" of our own imagination without sacrilege. Yet such Jesus-constructs proliferate today, even in the visible church, bearing no resemblance to the Messiah, because they are not rooted in Christ the *office-bearer* of Scripture. Many an imaginary Jesus is on offer. We have the positive-thinking psychological Jesus; the Marxist, liberationist Jesus; the hippie pacifist Jesus; the feminist or progressive Jesus; the social justice and LGBTQ-inclusive Jesus; the eco-warrior Jesus; the health and wealth, "your best life now" Jesus; but there is only one true Jesus Christ in the history of redemption in Scripture— the *office-bearer*—and the only one *true gospel* is about him.

In Jesus Christ we have *two names* joined and *two distinct natures* coming together uniquely. His singular office as *anointed one* was to do battle against Satan and all his works of sin, death and oppression at the turning point of the ages. His office was, according to Schilder, "To be the second Adam; that is, to establish a community of men, this time not of one blood, as a living soul, but from one Spirit as a quickening *pneuma*."[12] If then we are to understand Christ's *name*— and by it his *office*—we need to go back again to *Eden*, to the first Adam, for herein lies the key to the gospel.

The *first Adam* was made by God to be an *office-bearer*—a vice-regent in creation with rule and dominion in God's world in terms of God's Word and purpose. It was this office that was to *determine* Adam's actions and relationships. He was appointed to be God's fellow-worker (1 Corinthians 3:9). Our first parents' work in Eden was quite literally *liturgy*—service in and to the kingdom of God, which kingdom reaches over all the cosmos, including men and angels. The opening chapters of Genesis give us the basics of our first parents' task under God. They were to turn creation into a God-honouring and glorifying culture. They were to *cultivate* and *care* for creation, to rule in such a way as to reflect the character and rule of their Maker.

This created world was not pre-shrink-wrapped and microwavable, but fashioned in promise and in hope. Creation needed to be *developed*—its potentialities explored and resources creatively applied. The Edenic scene was therefore a *beginning*, not an ending

---

[12] Schilder, *Christ and Culture*, 18.

point, from which, with man as God's fellow-worker, the city of God would emerge full grown in the progress of the centuries. This required invention and every form of cultural activity, bound by God's ordinances and applying his principles for service. This cultural service was a mandate, not an end in itself, since man was bound to serve God's purpose with respect to the cosmos, "to kneel down now and presently, before his maker, in and together with a cosmos prepared by his own hand under God's providence, culturally engaged as he is in view of his own, but especially of God's Sabbath, into which he, man, has to enter,"[13] and, finally, place the fruit of all his activity at the feet of Christ. Life, in other words, was to be an *integral whole*, related in all its parts and functions to life and fellowship with God. This was all for the joy of knowing, loving, serving and glorifying God the Father with all that man has and is.

We have seen that Adam and Eve sinned and rebelled against God. They went instead about the task of "un-culture," and so propagated disintegration and decay. They abused their office and our race fell into ruin. Humanity sought instead to exercise autonomous rule and authority, to cultivate the earth for their own ends and serve themselves as their own god. The tools of culture became more important than the kingdom of God itself, and man's culture-making was absolutized. This resulted in the disintegration of life, the disordering, distortion, dereliction and diminution of all man's activities and relationships. Critically, this means that man is not only alienated from God, he seeks to *alienate God's world* from its Maker; to separate what God joins and join what God separates; to deny God's distinctions and create an illusory and socially-constructed reality of his own. The result is that he seeks to *separate religion and culture*, faith and science, God and the state from each other—for he seeks now the culture of Cain, not of Abel.

This means that, as far as man is concerned, God must have nothing to do with the real world, for there man must rebuild his own paradise in wilful rejection of God's verdict. People therefore deny the God-established unity of fact and meaning and insist on separate parts severed from the whole of God's creation and purpose. Put another way, sinful man now wants a *multi*-verse, not God's *uni*-verse,

---

[13] Schilder, *Christ and Culture*, 26.

with an integral meaning rooted in the triune God as Creator and sovereign. As such, the *antithesis* between the *seed of the woman* and the *seed of the serpent* develops in every area of life and thought. And, in the prolongation of time after the Fall, as gospel history differentiates the two cities, the development of this basic antithesis was inevitable. The scriptural worldview, therefore, unveils the fact that there is only one creation or nature, but there is a *two-fold* use of it. There is one earth, but there are *two different visions* for developing and shaping it. There is one cultural urge basic to humanity—to exercise dominion—but two distinct forms of cultural striving.

In the midst of man's futile efforts to remake himself as divine (as his own god), in the purposes of God, at the right moment, God sent forth the seed of the woman, his own Son the Messiah as the *second Adam* (1 Corinthians 15:45–48), to be the true *office-bearer* and so embody the office that man had been called to fulfill in the beginning. Jesus does this by perfect obedience. Christ therefore is situated in the gospel story as the one who *restores God's order*, bringing all things back to God by redeeming his new people, or new humanity, who recognize their calling "to serve God, in concrete life, to obey God in any function, to fulfill God's expressed will with all that is in us."[14]

So, in the gospel, Christ comes to make it possible for us to again fulfill our calling to serve God, to give back to him his world, developed and flourishing. That is why the Bible says that "God was in Christ reconciling the world unto himself" (2 Corinthians 5:19). His work in this regard was *juridical*, because man's problem was *ethical*, not *metaphysical*. He is the Redeemer into whose hands judgement is committed, not a philosopher who shares an abstract scheme for escaping reality. In life, the Messiah not only fulfills the *cultural role* of prophet, priest and king, just as Adam was called to do in the garden, but by his atoning death, he purchased *the right of renewal* of a new people, re-commissioned to be prophets, priests and kings in the service of God and to be his co-workers in the power of the Spirit, in the reconciling of all things in heaven and earth to God.

This is why the New Testament speaks of the *gospel* as the *gospel of the kingdom*, and of the kingdom of God as being in our midst in

---

[14] Schilder, *Christ and Culture*, 21.

the person of Christ the King. He is the Son of God, the Lord Messiah (office-bearer), and also the Son of Man, the *second king Adam*, invading history to recall us, by the gospel, to our true task of turning the creation into the culture or kingdom of God. The implications of this integral vision for history are glorious:

> In this administration of His own office and in the formation of those who are anointed together with Him (Christians) there comes about nothing less than a divine action (an action proceeding from the Father, Son and the Spirit) to conquer the world for God, by the Christ of God. "The earth is the Lord's and the fullness thereof" (Psalm 24:1). This conquest is a reconquest: the property is, as far back as has been destined from eternity, brought back to and restored in its proper relation to the owner. Christ connects the beginnings of the world with the end.[15]

THE SCOPE OF THE GOSPEL

We can see in this marvellous biblical perspective the exhilarating *scope* and *power* of the gospel in historical time. The frustration and futility of time, to which sin subjects us, is being *transformed* into fruitfulness by Christ's work. This vision moves us well beyond merely personal preoccupations with ourselves and our inward motions, our own sin and progress only, and directs us toward our calling to *serve the King*. The gospel knows nothing of escape from the world, but only of our service as priests for its renewal. The gospel is therefore not simply that we are saved *from our sins*, but that we are *delivered into* the kingdom of righteousness, now to serve God's purpose of righteous dominion as his image and office-bearers in Jesus Christ. The gospel sweeps up into its great symphony every movement of our daily work, our marriage and family, our vocations and callings. *Everything* that has been dominated by sin is now being transformed by the gospel. This gives the gospel a limitless application. Sandlin is very helpful on this point:

> Since God's work in Jesus Christ on the cross is designed to redeem everything presently under the domain of sin and since

---

[15] Schilder, *Christ and Culture*, 23.

this includes creation, creation should be redeemed. This means that all elements of culture, which is man's creative interaction with creation, including money and food and technology and education and the arts and politics presently burdened under the weight of sin are designed to be redeemed. Salvation isn't liberation from creation; it's liberation from sin. The gospel is calculated to redeem not just individuals but all human life and culture and creation.... The *good news*, is that God in Jesus Christ has dealt and is dealing decisively with the problem of sin and gradually reinstalling His righteousness in the earth. The gospel is that everything wrong in this world, God is setting right.[16]

This proclamation of salvation infuses the good news with a vast *cosmic scope*. It brings from every fibre of creation meaning and significance, and it challenges the compartmentalized, personalist, reductionist and escapist "gospel" that has deeply afflicted the contemporary church.

We have seen that the key to grasping this gospel reality lies in carefully plotting the journey from Eden to Christ. Christ's work was *prefigured* in Adam, whilst Adam's *created* sonship also reflects the greater Sonship of Christ, who is *eternally* the Son. Adam was a *co-ruler*, because he was made in the image of God the Son, who is ruler from all eternity. And yet, on the temporal horizon of history, Adam is a type of Christ, because he points to the One who, as the *perfect dominion man*, calmed the seas, commanded the storm and exercised total rule over creation. In Psalm 8 (paralleled in Hebrews 2:6–8), we are reminded of this calling, which is fulfilled perfectly in the work of Christ and to which he recalls us. Because of our sins, we forfeited relationship with God and, with it, our purpose of bringing creation into submission to its sovereign Lord. But, as John Barber points out,

By living the perfect life, and also by demonstrating absolute mastery over nature through miracles, Christ, the cultural man, fulfils God's dominion mandate flawlessly. His accomplishment

---

[16] Sandlin, "Reclaiming Culture," 5–6.

is made practical for us when by faith we place our trust on Christ for the forgiveness of sins. It is then that the vertical and horizontal connotations of our rebellion against a holy God are set aright. In Christ, man is restored in rich fellowship with God and also is returned to his co-dominion over the earth.[17]

THE ASCENSION AND SESSION OF CHRIST

In this missiological survey of the gospel from Eden, some readers might be thinking that there is perhaps triumphalistic overstatement in setting out the meaning and scope of the gospel as such a total victory over sin and its corruption and our restoration to that para-disal calling. Isn't salvation really just about being rescued from an evil world and going to be with Jesus? To address that inevitable question, we should note the importance of not only the *beginning* of this great gospel story, the earliest movement in the symphony of grace, but also the *concluding* crescendo in the glorification of Christ. We have observed that Christ is Alpha and Omega, the beginning and end. Christ indeed entered history over 2,000 years ago. He lived, died, was raised and ascended to heaven. So what can we say about the current status of the second Adam and the *implications* of this for the future?

As important as the doctrine of Christ's ascension is, the equally important truth of his *session*, of which the Bible and the creeds of the church speak, is often overlooked. The *session* of Christ is the reality of the perpetual presence of Jesus' *human nature* in the majesty and glory of heaven at the right hand of God the Father. That is to say that the *physical body* of Jesus is locally present in heaven, and so he sends his Holy Spirit into all the world in his stead. This truth links his resurrection and ascension in the gospels with the second coming for judgement as often set out in the epistles, because they are all part of the *total exaltation and victory of Christ*. As Paul writes, "he must reign until he puts all his enemies under His feet" (1 Corinthians 15:25). Because of his ascension and *session*, Christ is now ruling as God the Father's co-regent over the entire universe, as he wars in history to subject all things to himself.

---

[17] John Barber, *The Road from Eden: Studies in Christianity and Culture* (Bethesda: Academica Press, 2008), 534.

Prior to the *incarnation* of the last Adam, we have noted that the sons of Adam, under God's wrath, experienced loneliness and radical dislocation, expressed well by David in the Psalms, and drunk down to the dregs by Christ at the cross, when he experienced the agony of sin's dark curtain over God's face: "My God my God, why have you forsaken me?" (Psalm 22:1; Matthew 27:46). But, because of the death and resurrection of Christ, we are *restored* to an intimate communion with God that is, in principle, *closer* than Eden itself. This is because, in Jesus Christ, the resurrected office-bearer in heaven, *a Man*, sits in session with the triune God, warring against evil and sitting in judgement over it—for all judgement has been committed to the Son. Jesus' ascension and present rule are the "firstfruits" of all the new humanity, of the new creation, presented to God the Father (1 Corinthians 15:23). This is why Scripture tells us that *in Christ*, we are now seated *with Christ* in heavenly places (Ephesians 2:6). In light of our covenantal union with him, we participate now in his rule and victory. As such, the session of Christ is the exaltation of all his elect to their proper calling.

The church father Athanasius declared regarding the Pauline expression "highly exalted" that "the term in question, 'highly exalted' does not signify that the essence of the Word was exalted, for he was ever and is equal to God, but the exaltation is of the manhood."[18] Another noted church father, John Chrysostom, said of this same exaltation:

We who appeared unworthy of earth have been led up today into the heavens: we who were not worthy of the pre-eminence below have ascended to the Kingdom above: we have scaled the heavens: we have attained the royal throne, and that nature, on whose account the Cherubim guarded paradise, today sits above the cherubim.[19]

---

[18] Philip Schaff and Henry Wace, ed., *A Select Library of Nicene and Post-Nicene Fathers of the Christian Church.* vol. 4: *St. Athanasius: Select Works and Letters* (New York: Christian Literature Company, 1892), 330.

[19] John Chrysostom, cited in *The Foundations of Social Order: Studies in the Creeds and Councils of the Early Church*, ed. R.J. Rushdoony (Nutley, NJ: Presbyterian and Reformed, 1968), 137.

It is because of this incalculable privilege that we intercede today with God against evil and injustice, and it is in the ascension and session of the second Adam that we are assured of total victory. Temporal and spiritual enemies shall be made his footstool. By his regal power, Christ is subduing and shall subdue all things for his people and place them under our feet. At the end of history, in the final summing up, the great consummation of all things in Christ, he will see the travail of his soul and be satisfied (Isaiah 53:11). Everything will have been brought into subjection, willingly or unwillingly, and turned over to God the Father.

GOSPEL CULTURE
The gospel of the *kingdom of God*, the good news, thus extends its reach throughout all human history, from the time Adam was created and commissioned in a good creation and the first promise of reconciliation was made after the Fall, to the ascension, session and final judgement of Christ. The gospel is thus the *cosmic theatre* in which all of life is played out, either moving toward redemption or reprobation. The crescendo of this good news, the greatest movement in this symphony, is that the *office-bearer*, the man Jesus Christ, is on his throne, having made satisfaction for sins at the cross. He is now ruling and reigning and establishing his kingdom in the earth, reconciling all things in heaven and on earth to God. The theologian Daniel Strange has pointed out what this means for us as culture-makers:

As those united to Christ…*we inherit his story of relating to culture.* As the recapitulating second Adam, Jesus Christ is the man of culture par-excellence, anointed by the Spirit, demonstrating his perfect dominion over creation. His death deals with the divine wrath and curse, his resurrection is the firstfruits of the new creation. Christians are anointed by the Holy Spirit and, in their adoption as sons, are restored to take up the cultural mandate originally given to Adam. Our good works that cover every aspect of our individual, social and political lives, whilst never redeeming, are part of the redemptive kingdom. As done in Christ and by the Spirit, they are God's way of extending the kingdom in the present. As faithfully present ambassadors of Christ we actively proclaim his Lordship, taking every thought captive for him in anticipatory foretaste of the final consummation.[20]

That is the gospel. Since this mandate to have dominion and subdue all things under God existed even *prior to sin*, for us to avoid or reject that mandate of cultural labour in obedience to the Great Commission is sinful and in effect to be on strike against a gospel-centred life. Since Christ is also the very embodiment of all the treasures of wisdom and knowledge and all that is necessary for kingdom culture, for us to deny that we have a task on the earth to apply his salvation victory and lordship, his beauty and truth to all aspects of life and thought is to *renounce Christ*. It is for this reason that Klaas Schilder comments, "Every reformation that, driven by the Spirit of God, returns to the Scriptures, the Word of God, is at the same time a healing of culture."[21]

Christ is the king of the whole earth and we are his ambassadors. Because this gospel is true, our calling is *liturgy* (service as his royal priesthood), leading us to finally lay at God's feet all the fruits of our labours, the development of all our powers, in faithful adoration. This is our humble part in Christ's reconciliation and restoration of all things—the great summation. In that moment of unspeakable joy, when we place all that we are and have at his feet, having been faithful with the talents entrusted to us, we shall fully know that our Redeemer lives, the curse is ended and we shall reign with him forever. As one poet has aptly concluded:

New Eden comes
And all else passes.
The Hills grown old with time
Shall see their youth again.
The cold stone walls of Jericho
Around the heart of ancient man
Shall fall before the trumpets blow

---

[20] Daniel Strange, "Faithful Presence: A Theology for the Trenches?" in *Revisiting Faithful Presence: To Change the World Five Years Later*, ed. Collin Hansen (Deerfield: The Gospel Coalition, 2015), 47–56, 52.

[21] Schilder, *Christ and Culture*.

As victors seize the land.
The time that comes
Beats with the loudest drums.
Creation has but one conclusion.[22]

---

[22] Rushdoony, "New Eden," in *The Luxury of Words*, 107.